**What People Are Saying About
Wendy Lee Baldwin and This Book:**

"Wendy Lee Baldwin's, *Healing Your Soul In A Chaotic World: Defying the Odds of Sanity and Survival*, is a wonderful testimonial to how we can find healing from even the most frightening of human conditions if we continue to believe in the power of the human connection. Baldwin takes us on a harrowing journey through various illnesses and self-destructive behavior to show how her faith in humanity and her desire to use her experience to help others eventually brought her to a place where healing was possible. This book has true power."

— Russell Rowland, author of
In Open Spaces and *High and Inside*

"A story courageously written…a life courageously lived…an outcome with many inherent lessons of transformation and healing. Wendy Lee Baldwin's journey is a powerful one, and a lesson to those of us seeking transformation within forgiveness."

—Alan Roth - Musician/Author of
Fields Beyond the Known

"This powerful and dynamic book engages and encourages readers to value their life, to live it with intent together with a mindful and purposeful spirit."

—Susan Friedmann, CSP, international best-selling author of
Riches in Niches: How to Make it BIG in a small Market

"Wendy's perceptiveness, compassion and her understanding of suffering at a soul level combined with her ability to really listen enable her to be of real assistance to other people and help them achieve wholeness as she has. This story of her growing up, vividly brought to life, provides an inspirational example of what can be achieved through strength of spirit, total forgiveness and love. I am so happy to have been a part of her life."

— Cindy Reed, Artist/Author of
If I Could Go Outside With My Eyes Closed

"Who hasn't had a painful or humiliating event that will pop into your head just when you are happy and feeling good? Remove that painful experience FOREVER. This holistic approach to healing buried pain is rapidly becoming more mainstream and it works! Be open and trust the process that Healer Wendy Lee Baldwin offers. The self-guided tools at the end of this book will help you transition out of old pain and start stepping into your power right away."

— Lisa Montgomery, Business owner
Luxurious Fishing Vacations

"Wendy has delivered an easy to read but vivid account of a tragic childhood that inspired her to not only heal herself, but also to assist others in their healing. While her story is heart wrenching, it isn't about dwelling on the emotional injuries but rather it's about feeling and releasing emotional damage. She has courageously shared her journey in hopes that her readers will be inspired to heal whatever emotional or physical pain they are currently living with."

— Patti Rea Donovan,
Business Executive

"If you need hope and are tired of isolating yourself because of the abuse you lived through, you must read Wendy Lee Baldwin's book. She will hold your hand along the way and guide you from anger, resentment and chaos to peace, love, forgiveness and happiness. Inspiring and empowering!"

— Joy Alboro, Business owner of In Joyful Living

"I know, first-hand, from early childhood, the feeling of numbness, not being good enough and worthless. When the pain is great enough it's time for change. The methods Wendy Lee Baldwin uses to heal her life will also work for you, to enable you to get your life back. The secrets to healing and transforming your life are forgiveness – of self and others, gratitude and love. The powerful tools at the end will help you get yourself started NOW to become empowered."

— Stephania Gibb, Author of *"Don't Throw Your First Born (or Yourself) Off The Balcony" Seven Easy Steps for First Time Parents.*

"Sometimes the human experience is one riddled with pain and confusion, but sometimes it is those very things that cause the greatest shake-up and shake out of what's not working in our lives. These times clear up space for the good stuff to come in. They are the catalyst to our transformation. In this book, Wendy shares her experiential journey as an example of how to evolve into a place of truth, inner peace, and to step into the power of your own becoming. It's a must read to help you align with your joy!"

— Nicole Gabriel, Author of *"Finding Your Inner Truth"*
and "Stepping Into Your Becoming"

"This book holds up to its truths because it's personable and you can relate to a lot of issues described because it is a human experience. I found it very relatable and open to a lot of emotional and traumatic events that have happened to me. A must read!"

— Mwati Mwila –Poet-Author of
"The Sweet Surrender of Love and Nature

"The secrets to healing and transforming your life are forgiveness, gratitude and love. This book delivers this with a punch. You won't want to put it down till the end."

— Patrick Snow, Publishing Coaching and International
Best Seller Author of *Creating Your Own Destiny*

"I have known Wendy since 2003 and have learned so much from her as a friend, person, and coach. I do know about some of her personal struggles, which having seen how she has come out of them victoriously with such a passion for helping others—leaves me in awe. It restores my faith in the human spirit."

—Leisa Good, Business owner - PowerfullyPurposedForSuccess.
com and GBSVirtualOfficeSolutions.com

"Not one of us has made it down the road of life without some adversity. If you are looking for hope, want someone to understand you, and your journey, then Wendy Baldwin has the help you really need. Join her as she shares the lessons she has learned on the road to healing and overcoming. She will get you back on your journey!"

— Jim R. Jacobs, LCSW, Author of *Driving Lessons For Life:
Thoughts on Navigating Your Road to Personal Growth*

AN UNCONVENTIONAL BLUEPRINT FOR LETTING GO AND TRANSFORMING YOUR LIFE.

HEALING YOUR SOUL IN A CHAOTIC WORLD

DEFYING THE ODDS OF SANITY AND SURVIVAL

WENDY LEE BALDWIN

AVIVA
PUBLISHING
New York

*"Healing does not mean the damage never existed.
It means the damage no longer controls our lives."*

Daily Dose

To Donovan, Megan, Hailee and Scarlett –
The lights of my life

And in loving memory of Grandma

ACKNOWLEDGMENT

This book is dedicated to everyone in my life: Past, present and future. Thank you for helping me become who I AM today. Without you being a vessel to reflect back to me what I needed to learn and heal in order to grow, I would not have experienced my soul's expansion or remembered why I'm here.

I'm deeply grateful to all of those who stood beside me, believed in me and loved me when I couldn't love myself. I would not be alive today if it wasn't for you and the whispers of the Universe/Source encouraging me to "hang on a little longer." You, the parade of doctors and healers who worked with me were all answers to my prayers. Thank you for crossing my path and walking with me for the length of time that your services were needed. You not only helped me heal myself, but taught me what I needed to learn in order to become a healer, coach and safe place for others to land who are starving for help.

A special note of gratitude goes out to all of the cutting edge, modern scientists who prove that our cells store memories. Because of your brilliance, we now know, without a doubt, that every event, conversation and emotion that has happened in our life is imprinted in these cells and our brain. Everything is available for recall when accessed.

Some of my memories come from conscious recollection. Others like those in Chapter 1, and older subconscious recollections, as well as past life events are relived through the power of key energy releasing processes. We are all energy and with our lives stored as such, the archives are accessible anytime one is ready to open that vault.

Mahalo nui loa to everyone who helped me with this book…my labor of love…and gift to the world…you helped me make this possible. A HUGE shout out goes to my beloved big sister, Cindy

Reed. You are the best big sister anyone could ask for. You wore many hats as you helped me get this manuscript to print. Not only did you catch a shameful amount of typing errors before going to press, you also gave me your unbiased editorial input. You even created an original oil masterpiece that encapsulates our story. I will figure out a way to show off your stunning artistic skills to the masses since it wasn't used in this book as originally planned. Your love is always with me.

I'm grateful for my editor, Russell Rowland, for encouraging me to get my story written, helping me flush out scenes that needed expanding and guiding me where needed.

A special shout out goes to Patrick Snow, my mentor and book savior. Thank you, Patrick for guiding me in making this a bigger and better tool in order to help more people. I love that we both have the same goal of helping mankind transform their life and step into their greatness.

INTRODUCTION

Did you know that 100% of humans have been betrayed either though divorce, losing a job, jilted by a lover, abused or sexually assaulted? Been lied to, robbed or bullied? Did you also know that depression, thoughts of suicide, dis-ease in the body, weight issues and anxiety can be linked as a result of betrayal down to your core?

How many ways have you experienced betrayal? More than one? More than two? What about the emotions attached to betrayal…. Do you feel abandoned, rejected or unloved? Grief stricken?… Shame? What other emotions do you secretly battle with, year after year? The truth is, all of this *hurts*.

How do you mask the pain? Do you wash it down with alcohol, trip out on drugs, stuff yourself with junk food …ease the pressure by cutting yourself? Or do you numb yourself while recklessly racking up your credit cards, buying stuff you don't really need (but justify)…all in hopes of filling the empty space deep down inside your chest and gut?

I know what it feels like to be betrayed. Over and over. I understand what it does to the physical, mental and spiritual self. I understand wanting to commit suicide….To feel like the biggest mistake God ever created. Worthless. Filled with anger, rage, resentment and hatred…Feeling powerless. That's how I lived every second, of every day of my life for over 50 years.

I know what it feels like to slug through the day feeling numb and detached…living from the ceiling, as if watching yourself from outside your body... Simply surviving and on guard for the next attack. For most of my life, I didn't even understand that was how I felt. Why? Because of overwhelm and not knowing how to put feelings into words. Destructive emotions simply ran in the background of my nervous system, like a hidden computer virus…always eating away at me.

Through my story that you are about to read, you will witness how trauma effects the psyche, the body and spirit. You will also be exposed to unconventional, perhaps radical, ways to heal on the soul and cellular level. You will watch as a dying soul is revived and brought back to life, ready to transform and take life to a higher level.

Actually, even though the events happened in my life, this is really your *story* too. Notice what parts you identify with and take comfort that you are no longer alone. Know that someone understands what your pain feels like. Take comfort knowing that someone empathizes with your plight.

The human spirit is unstoppable when there is hope. This story is laced with pockets of hope to keep you going. You will see that healing from your deepest, darkest secrets, your most destructive experiences, is possible. You will understand that fortitude and clarity turns dreams into reality.

Notice the feelings of transmuting self-sabotage into beauty that radiates out to all those you touch. You will understand that My

Truth is Your Truth…That you are worthy of your greatest dreams, endless love and that you matter. Best of all, the negativity - the lies and betrayal - that created your level of dis-ease is healable when you are ready.

Yes, you can heal the festered wounds of betrayal. You can let go of the rage, hatred, resentment and shame….regardless of the depths of your suffering. Age doesn't matter either. You're never too old or too young to let go and feel better. Yes, you can mend your shattered heart and soul. Yes, you can transform your life and BE HAPPY beyond your wildest dreams.

Sometimes healing is fast and simple. Other times it's like riding a roller coaster on steroids. Sometimes you have to crack the wound wide open, peel back the layers and dig deep. Then stitch yourself back up. Sometimes it's scary and overwhelming. But unleashing the buried torment is always worth the time and effort.

My story is your story because we share the human experience. Perhaps your details and events are more severe than mine. Hopefully not… May this time of sharing bring you peace knowing someone understands you if you feel lost and alone…encouragement in searching for your own inner love and peace. And the endurance to never, ever, ever give up. Stay focused and you will find what you seek.

Healing starts with awareness, desire and action. The next level is forgiveness, gratitude and love. Then you have what your soul yearns for…Lives for….Freedom!

Because of the trauma I experienced and determination to heal, I became a powerful energy/holistic healer. People come to me because they know they are safe with their deepest, darkest secrets. They know that I hold sacred space with them and respect where they are in their healing journey, who they are, and hold their hand every step of the way. People thank me for helping them change their life. They are grateful that they had the courage to take action and ask for help. I am also a certified Wellness coach and Certified Master Spiritual coach, and motivational speaker.

It's my goal to bring awareness to the greatness inside you. It's okay if you feel resistance or fear to change. That's normal. You've lived with pain for so long that it is a familiar part of who you are. Perhaps even a vital part of your identity. Stepping out from behind the shadows and saying, "Hey! Stop the madness!" will come when you're ready.

Living a busy life, juggling kids, work and family expectations might not leave much time or energy for you. Life is chaotic. However, I invite you, dear friend, to take a deep breath, ask your heart and soul what she/he needs for expansion. Listen and follow your inner calling.

I hope to encourage you to live life large, with gusto and as the expansive, magnificent Being that you are. It's time for you to speak up and let your silenced voice be heard. When you are ready, I'd be honored to be your mentor and help you transform your life. You can count on me to hold your hand and guide you along the way.

Are you ready to step outside your comfort zone and onto the platform of a magnificent, elevated life? Are you ready to reclaim your power? Be unstoppable and soar to great heights? If so, declare today as your day of shedding the scars and wounds of the past. And start living! Let's hold hands and dive right in. At the end of this book, you will find helpful tools to get you started letting go and transitioning.

As you will see, the names of the people in this book are replaced by the role they played. A few of the locations are changed too. This is done to protect privacy. Some of the events are not necessarily the main focus, but rather what I learned from the experiences and how they affected my mental and physical health.

This is not a "Tell-All" of who did what to wrong me. Instead, this is our story of gratitude, self-discovery and finally opening up to self-love, and being unbelievably happy, healed and alive…against the odds.

The first fourteen chapters are the retelling of my story. If you are eager to jump in, start healing and transforming your life right away, please skip ahead to chapters 16-19.

Always remember this…If I can do it…you can do it too!

Love,

Wendy Lee Baldwin

CONTENTS

"Until you heal the wounds of your past, you are going to bleed.
You can bandage the bleeding with food, with alcohol,
with drugs, with work, with cigarettes, with sex; but eventually,
it will all ooze through and stain your life.
You must find strength to open the wounds,
stick your hands inside,
pull out the core of the pain that is holding you in your past,
the memories, and make peace with them."

— Iyanla Vanzant, ***Yesterday, I Cried***

PROLOGUE

Fluorescent lights sting my eyes as I bat them open. The inside of my head spins around as I struggle to make out where I am. Blue blanket. Husband in a chair to my left. A garbled male voice coming from somewhere. A deep breath in and my eyes grasp seconds of recognition. More males. Two this time. The tone sends a jolt through my system. Something is wrong. "Focus," I tell myself. I remember now what is happening. I'm in the hospital. My eyes focus more steadily now and my hearing becomes clearer in spurts.

DrK stands in the doorway; his neatly combed dark hair is a strong contrast to the white lab coat that protects his street clothes beneath. His eyes lock onto mine and that connection speaks trouble. My energy struggles to stay alert. And I must. The vibrato of the voices tells me so. Pay attention now. Husband looks at me. I'm unable to read what his green eyes say. Back to DrK. The fog is lifting more now but the muscles in my neck flounder and my head wobbles. DrK says that my colon is very diseased. He stopped the colonoscopy short because he could not get the scope up all the way through the inflamed tube that is my garbage disposal system. He and Husband exchange words and look at each other as I struggle to stay alert. DrK seems angry at me. Or is he scared like I am now too?

DrK leaves and Husband does his best to help guide my weakened arms and legs inside the necessary openings of my shirt and pants. He pulls socks up over my cold, exposed feet and ties the laces of my white Avia cross trainers. We manage the 10-minute drive home where I collapse and melt into my brown recliner. I stay here, practically immobile until the anesthesia filters out of my system and I become fully alert.

I look at the glossy colored photos of my colon. Rage, fear, and the threat of a colostomy bag glares back at me. This can't be happening. I'm doing everything I know to heal my body. To heal my life. But the more I heal my emotional self, the more my body defies me.

Three months earlier DrK removed multiple polyps and a mass. He feared cancer back then, explaining that my body was one cell turn away from the inevitable. Professionals proclaim that there is no cure for the disease that has robbed me of good health, my freedom, my joy. I hate this disease. DrK's fears are even deeper now. He wasn't able to explore and see what grew back in the rotting lining of my toxic waste dump.

He is angry at me because earlier I refused a powerful drug therapy that he prescribed. The drug scares me because of what it does to other organs. The expense would put us over the cliff financially and I cannot take money away from the family for just me. That would be selfish. The odds are greatly against me, now more than ever.

My deeply rooted belief since the fourth grade that God would not give us a disease unless he also gave us a cure has always been my driving force, pushing me forward in healing myself. But now my faith starts to waver. What if I'm wrong and the doctors are right? What if they've always been right? What if I'm crazy to believe that I have the power, the knowledge and endurance to heal myself?

Is what I consider my inner knowing actually stubborn ego? If so, will it cause me to die trying to save what is left of my life force? If so, I need to fulfill my big dream and move to Hawaii as soon as possible.

Tick tock I'm running out of clock. This place is killing me. If I'm going to die anyway, I will die where I started life. I will surrender my ashes to the wind. There will be no grave stone for me because I don't believe one is necessary. I will become a faded memory. And I will no longer endure my inner torture; my cross to bear. The hell I created for myself that I could not overcome…

But at least my soul will be free…at last.

Chapter 1

THE DISPOSABLE CHILD

We lie together, curled up in the fetal position. The hard wooden floor beneath us braces us as Father strikes us, blow after blow. We are trapped and must endure his wrath over a crime I do not understand. The only barrier separating me from a direct hit is the safety inside mother's womb. The cramped quarters of our 42' foot timber fishing boat, the *Maile Flo*, houses Mother, Father, Sister and Brother. With a double bed on one side and bunks for my siblings on the other side, a tiny kitchenette and a toilet that has to be pumped by hand, it doesn't leave any room for me, the pending newborn.

Shock and terror surge through Mother's veins. Loathing for the man she vowed to love till death. Rage and hatred towards the man who is striking her down like a naughty child merge with me and become my own. My tiny, delicate organs and nervous system take the jolt of the chemical poison and bury deep within my cell memory. My tiny form is on high alert. Danger! Danger! An invisible switch is flipped and I am ready to run, to battle, to defend my right to be alive but I have nowhere to go. I'm stuck and so I must hide.

Now terror strikes my heart and a part of me freezes. A new message seeps into awareness. The message fully engulfs me that I am unworthy of love. I am a mistake that must be disposed of. I don't deserve to live. The world is not big enough for one more mouth to feed. I am a burden. God's biggest mistake. Some mistakes can be erased. And I am one of those.

Mother cries out but her tears are unanswered. The sway of the tide ebbing and flowing rocks our boat even as we are tethered to the dock in Ala Wai harbor. I like the motion and calm down as Mother begins calming down too.

I am too young to understand the language that is spoken outside the darkness where I live. Muffled noise filters through the fluid that keeps me bathed in warmth, as does the vibration behind the sounds. Mother's worries are my worries. Her fears are my fears even though I don't fully understand what we are afraid of or worried about.

I grow bigger and bigger and now the dark, warm, wet space that is my home is too small for me. Even though I'm restricted in movement, I'm not ready to leave yet. I have no idea where I'd be going anyway. Instinctually I know that I must move on at some point though.

Energy shifts and confusion hits. Something is happening. Mother is panicking and yelling. I am on high alert but can't run. Can barely move about inside my cramped quarters. We are suddenly weightless and we are flying through the air. Now we are sinking and Mother is struggling to swim. Brother fell off the side of the boat and he will drown if we don't save him. We stroke one arm followed by the other, bringing us closer to his small body that has somehow managed to get trapped under the wooden walkway.

We find him floating on his back like an expert swimmer taking a rest at the end of a race. He is alive! Mother tucks his toddler size body under one of her arms, her other arm frantically paddling the three of us to the back of our boat. We are all too heavy for her to carry and climb the ladder back up onto the *Maile Flo* to safety. Mother yells out for help. A man arrives and drags soaking wet bodies up and out of the water. Mother is frantic even though we are saved. Her anxiety makes me frantic. I have to get out of here! I flip upside down and press hard against the exit door. *Let me out!*

Mother catches her breath and does her best to calm down for a short while, but I don't. She is relieved that Brother did not drown. But her relief is too late for me. She bends over in pain as I insist that it's time for me to burst out of hiding. It's time for me to run away from this place. Life is not safe. Who am I? Why did I come here? The unknown terrifies me. I don't understand what is beyond this passage way. All I know is that I must make a move. Now!

**

Mother and I race to the hospital with the help of a friend's car. Father drives and drops us off in the care of people we don't know then returns home to Sister and Brother. Sister is 2 ½ years old. Brother is barely a year. They cannot take care of themselves any better than I can. Mother and I are tired from so much energy spent. She needs rest but I refuse to stay inside her another moment.

I emerge from the narrow, tight passageway and find myself in the hands of a doctor. He passes me to a nurse who cleans me and puts a cloth diaper on my bare bottom. The room is cold and I don't understand what is happening. A nurse carries me somewhere away from the others and lies me down. She walks away and I am alone in this new space.

Where is Mother? I want Mother! I cannot find her. A sound

scratches from my insides and pierces my ear drums. Mother does not come for me. She is nowhere to be found. My cries for her go unanswered. Something hard but squishy is forced into my mouth. I close my lips around the mysterious object and my instinct to suckle takes over. I gulp down the liquid but it hurts my tummy. I cry more. Other babies like me are in the same room yet I feel alone. Why did I come here?

The cooing and cuddling of the nurses does not replace the empty space inside me that longs for Mother. She protected me while I developed from an accidental meeting of sperm and egg to my birth but now she is gone. I am a bad child. I must be punished. God is angry at me and disappointed in me. I am his biggest mistake.

It's three days now since Mother and I parted ways. She finally comes for me. She takes me home to our boat. It's the first time I feel the expanse and constriction of the reality of our home. The ebb and flow of the water rocks me to sleep. I will rest while I can.

**

Something is wrong. The air is static with worry. Fear. Anguish. Something happened to Sister while Mother and I were in the hospital. The friend who took care of Siblings harmed her in horrific ways. Guilt drapes my newborn self like a suffocating blanket. This is my fault. Someone blames me. If I had not been born, then Sister would be safe. "I am so sorry", is all I can feel but the words do not form. They can't. Instead, I cry and bury the guilt inside my heart and every cell of my body. Yes, I am to blame. God was wrong in making me. How will I live with knowing what I did to Sister? I want to go back home to wherever I came from. This new place does not want me.

**

My eyes see blackness all around. "Mother, where are you?" my two-week-old self cries out. She does not respond so I call her again. Whack, whack, whack on my little back. Father's angry hand tells me to leave Mother alone. To leave all of them alone. His hand stops sending jolting pain inside me but invisible wounds surround my heart where scars will form. My cries morph into whimpers until at last I am able to silence my voice. I'm sorry for being born.

**

A hot breeze blows but it's not from the ocean. Something is happening again. A man arrives. He holds me, looks me over. Coos. Smiles. He is warm and happy. He doesn't know what I've done to Sister and I won't tell him. He stays with us and is eager to help take care of me. Mother holds on to me as often as she can. She sings to me. Her angelic voice quiets my worries. She cries too. Her sadness makes me sad. I don't understand why she is so sad. My tummy hurts a lot. She holds me more. She holds me close as if she doesn't want to let go. As if we are one again.

The man and my family walk to Ala Moana park. I sleep on a blanket on the ground below a giant shady tree and another blanket covers me, keeping me warm. Siblings play in the park as I sleep. Someone takes a black and white photo to preserve this moment in time. We all leave the park but our energetic imprint is left behind marking the spot like an invisible signature or branding in the ground. The imprint Sister and I leave behind is the strongest.

But wait…where are we going? The man is taking me away from Mother. He is taking me away from Father. He is taking me away from Siblings and my section of the harbor. We board a plane and I cry. What is going on? I don't recognize the women who take turns holding me, fussing over me in an effort to stop me from calling out to Mother. They don't understand that my tummy is in a giant knot and I don't understand what is happening. I want Mother but she doesn't find me. Mother's energy told me that she wanted a child to cuddle. One who liked to be touched and hugged. That's me! Not Sister or Brother. She found what she was looking for in me. So why did she let me go?

I am angry! No one is listening to me! My energy runs out and I must sleep but something brews inside me. Hatred. Resentment. Grudge. I loathe Father with every cell of my body. This is his doing. He didn't want me from the beginning. He hoped I'd die early on but I didn't. I lived and now I'm going to pay for it. And so will he. He won't get away with disposing of me. I will forget him but he won't forget me. I'll haunt him every day of his life. Not because I am an evil child. Oh, no, this has nothing to do with actions on my part. Even monsters can't hide or forget their dirty deeds. And Mother will pay too, because she gave away the wrong child.

Chapter 2

THE MOMMY GAME

NewMommy coos at me and smiles. We don't know each other yet but I place my life in her hands. NewDaddy grins ear to ear when he sees me. They fumble here and there with me but overall the three of us do the best we can. I cry a lot. My tummy hurts. Milk from the bottle twists and turns inside me, and I can't stop it. My once tiny body that I had no control over is growing bigger and bigger. I learn to smile and laugh.

A snapshot is taken of me today as I splash in the faucet outside. My red two-piece swimsuit shows off my bare belly. My nearly bald head soaks up the sun. Today I smile as I cool myself off from the Tennessee heat. It's my birthday and I eat cake in my fancy high chair that has a large tray to hold me in my seat. Cake is good. Life is good.

*****

NewMommy is not here. She vanished. Grandma is with me instead. Daddy, Grandma, and I are here but I don't understand where we are. A strange man sits in this room. He wears black and smiles at me. He holds me in his arms and looks me over. He likes me. I like him. He hands me back to Daddy. They exchange words, but I don't know what they're saying. Grandma speaks too. The three of them are serious but not angry so I don't worry or cry. Just be quiet. The three of us leave. Still, NewMommy does not come.

**

California is our home now. Sunny days and the freedom of my tricycle calls me outside. Grandma tells me not to ride my tricycle on the road. It's too steep of a hill, she says. We live at the top. I hear her warning but the road calls my name and I must do my best to peddle over the black surface that holds little rocks together like glue. Something catches under my tire and in a flash I tip over. Bam! My knees slap the hard ground. Blood oozes from my skin. Screams burst from my lips. Grandma runs to my rescue. She tends to my flesh and is grateful I am okay.

Grandma loves me, this I know. I love her. She is my mommy but I'm not allowed to call her that. Daddy insists that I must call her Grandma. I don't want to though because she is my heart. And my heart says she is Mommy.

We tell secrets, snuggle, and she scratches my back exactly how I like it. She knows her special touch helps me fall asleep at night. We watch silly people on her black and white t.v. I do not understand how big people can fit inside a box in the living room and make us laugh. But it works.

Grandpa is here too but he walks out of the door in the morning and comes back in time for dinner. Daddy does the same. Grandpa and Daddy make me smile, but it's Grandma who I cling to. Daddy says he wants a boy. A son. I know what a boy is. One lives next door to our single wide trailer. He climbs the steps to our porch and knocks on the metal door and asks Grandma if Winkydink can come out and play. That's me. He can't say my name but I don't care. I like it when he comes to visit.

Even though I don't see Daddy much, I know he loves me. But, would he love me more if I were a boy? Yes, I think so. I don't know how I know this but something inside me tells me boys are liked better than girls. This mixes me up because Grandma does not make me feel this way. Only Daddy.

Grandma shows me how to hold a sewing needle and to run thread through the tiny hole that is called the "eye". She has trouble seeing the hole so she lets me help her. She ties thread in a knot at the end and weaves the needle and thread through fabric, patching holes where toes dig their way out of socks. She shows me how to sew with a machine that makes two pieces of fabric stick together and form into dresses for me.

I take Grandma's lessons and use them to stitch up a hole in my shirt. In and out, in and out, I carefully guide the needle. Pull too hard on the thread and it makes the material pucker. Don't do that. Grandma encourages me to keep practicing my sewing and tells me I do a good job.

We bake pies together and giggle as we work. We mix flour that floats on particles of air as it lands in the bowl. Mix in something goopy that holds the flour together. Add water and salt. Mix together. Roll tender dough out on the Formica table. The rolling pin is a bit much for Grandma to handle alone so I help her. Raisin pie. Fried apple pies. Tiny pies for me baked in silvery pans. I'm the only one who gets a pie of my own. Grandma always makes one just for me. We laugh. We sing. Invisible cords connect us to each other and cannot be broken. We are like one.

⁎⁎

We move away from California to a place called Washington. Something is wrong with Grandma. Bright lights glare and bounce off the walls making my stomach scrunch up inside, and an alarm screams from my insides out. Grandma lies on her back in the narrow bed while grownups fuss over her. She is sick but no one knows what's wrong. Confusion swirls around me and I am hungry for Grandma to tell me she is okay and that we'll be going home soon.

I'm led by the hand to an elevator and someone pushes a button to make us move. Wait!...Grandma isn't with us!...We must get her. I cannot leave without her! Long screams burst from my gut and I refuse to leave without Grandma. Someone is telling me that we have to leave her, so she can get better. I don't believe this. She will die if I leave her here. We are not to be apart. One cannot live without the other. At least I cannot live without her.

People who disappear from my life do not come back. Grandma will be lost forever if I leave her behind. In this moment I vow to fix Grandma by taking on her pain. Her pain is now my pain. I will carry this burden for her. She is my everything. I am nothing without her. This is my secret. My insides clench tight and I cry out Grandma's name. But she can't run to me. She can't wrap her warm arms around me and assure me everything is okay. Because it's not. She is helpless against unseen forces that are bringing her down. And so am I.

I'm pulled inside the small, slow moving elevator against my will. The door closes, separating me from Grandma, trapping me in a space I resist. There is no way back to her. I'm not strong enough to fight or open the doors myself. I give in and ride to another area where we must exit to the car. Tears soak my face, grief tainted breaths catch in my lungs as I continue to wail uncontrollably. Women wearing long black robes and pointy hats walk past me. They look like giant penguins but I know they are nuns like on t.v. which means nothing to me. Their faces tell me they wish they could mend the shattered heart inside me, but they can't.

Daddy assures me that I'll see Grandma again but I don't believe him. He wants me to stop crying but pain demands to express itself the only way I know how right now. We pull out of the parking lot and drive the slow path to an empty home. This is my fault. I wonder if I somehow made Grandma sick. Yes, I believe so. And now I must be punished for what I've done.

**

I run around the yard like a speedy racer, my feet hit the green grass with every stride. Our back yard is big enough for me to jump and skip and be free. A wooden fence tells me how far I can go and when to turn around. My long, thin, wispy hair flies in the breeze that I create with my energy. Our small yellow bungalow with a detached single car garage is just big enough for five-year-old me and Daddy. A giant tree gives shade and a place for Daddy to lean against as he smokes.

Grandma and Daddy sit on the back porch, watching me laugh and call their attention. I stop in front of them and wriggle my hips back and forth and wave my arms side to side. Daddy calls me his little hula girl. He tells me that he found me under a coconut shell on the beach in Hawaii. This makes me feel special, because by now I know everyone else comes by stork.

Someone broke into our garage last night. Daddy tells Grandma they busted a window and we go see for ourselves. Canned food is missing. Someone was hungry but not any more. I don't care much about this and carry on in my own imagination taking myself someplace magical where babies grow on beaches and many other faraway places that my mind takes me.

Daddy lets me pick out a dog at a special shelter. Lots and lots and lots of dogs crowd around the door where we look at them through a window. Every dog seems to say, "Take me home!" but I can only have one. I choose a small brown one with long silky ears and short legs. I call her Taffy. We are in love.

**

Grandma lives nearby but is not able to care for me like before. A nice lady I call Grandma2 lives down the road. We like each other, and she lets me stay with her sometimes while Daddy works. She's not my grandma but I call her that. She is fun but by dinner time we're both ready for me to leave. I stare at the cars as they zoom past on the freeway behind her house. I carefully watch for our blue and white Volkswagen bus. Several trick me into thinking they are Daddy. Finally he comes before I cry too much. My heart misses him when he is gone. He is gone more than I see him.

Another lady takes care of me. I like her brown hair and friendly smile. She is nice at first but she steals my paper bag full of pennies off my dresser. Theft is a new personal experience for me, and I don't like it. It leaves an empty spot inside me. Having someone steal my prized money is different than when someone stole food from us out of the garage before. This time I learn a lesson. I learn not to be excited about having much money because someone will take it away. I also discover that not all women are as nice as they pretend to be.

BabySitter comes next. So does her baby daughter. We all love each other right away. I want BabySitter as my mommy and ask Daddy if she can be. He says no, but I stay hopeful. We watch Romper Room before school every day. She sews me a Halloween costume and fuss-es over it until I give her a final approval. She lets me watch her baby for a few minutes. This makes me feel like a big, important girl. She tells me I do a good job with babies. I am sad when she leaves every day. But my heart reopens as she steps back into my day.

BestFriend lives a short walk from me. We are practically sisters. Her hair is lighter than mine and she is prettier than me, but I don't care. Her mother is nice when I visit. We expertly play our favorite recess game of Say, Say, Ol' Playmate. Our voices carry loud enough for us to hear but not others around us. We giggle and move our hands back and forth, front and back as we clap along to the tune. We stay in our little world, shutting out others.

Recess is something I am good at. The freedom of being outside in-stead of surrounded by walls makes me happy. But we must go back inside and sit on wooden chairs and learn how to do hard things. Like count.

Teacher calls a boy to the front of the room. An abacus sits on the desk up high so everyone can see. Wooden beads move along wires to help him count. He says numbers I don't recognize. He stops and we clap. Teacher tells him he did well. It's my turn. I hesitate with so many eyes on me. This makes me feel funny inside, like something is fluttering around and my voice struggles to pass over my tongue.

I move the beads across the wire from one end to the other. My lips count one, two, three, all the way up to nine. My brain stops then scrambles with numbers others used before me but none calls out to be true. I turn and look at Teacher. She smiles and tells me to ask others for help. Classmates volunteer their hands in the air. I am to pick one and see who is right. If they are right, then I am right. Who do I pick? Him. I'll pick him. He shouts a number and I believe him. His answer is now my answer. Teacher tells me I am wrong. The crowd laughs, and I slink back to my chair. My desk is too small for me to hide under. Now I know that I am not one of the smart kids. I am not smart enough to understand math, which is something about numbers.

What I know for sure is that I like recess and nap time. Sometimes I am really good at *Show and Tell* too. It is said that I have a good imagination. Returning home and playing with BestFriend and Taffy is what I'd rather do. They are my only friends and the only ones I need.

**

Daddy and I drive down I-5, me sitting beside him, feeling like the big girl that I am. We like sharing stories, being silly and singing songs on the road. Little Bunny Foo Foo always makes us giggle. I ask Daddy lots of questions like how are we to know what we are supposed to do in life. How does life work? He tells me that God has a blueprint for each of us. We follow what He has outlined for us. Daddy says that some people get a nice, happy, easy life. Some of us don't. We just have to accept what God has planned for us.

The eyes inside my head create a map made just for me, but I can't see where the map leads beyond right now. I ponder and wonder what God has in store for me. In some ways this seems right that we'd have a plan outlined for us, but in other ways it doesn't seem fair. What if we don't like what God has planned for us?

**

I pass kindergarten! This means I get to move on to first grade like my classmates. This means I get to be like a big kid. Daddy says we are moving again. I must let someone else take care of Taffy from now on. We are moving in with people I don't know. They live far away from here in a city named Fife but they will help take good care of me.

Why are we moving? BestFriend can't come with me. Neither can BabySitter or her baby. Just me and Daddy moving in with strangers. We lived with strangers before like the nice lady in the big fancy house. We lived upstairs in a bedroom with a tiny kitchen and a bathroom down the hall. Her giant poodle liked me, and I liked her. The lady liked me too and gave me a birthday cake once. But this time, living with strangers will be different. We won't have our own little space. We will share in a house. It's too much to jumble around in my head.

But first, BabySitter must say goodbye. I wave as my security and happy life back out of the driveway, leaving me behind. I become untethered as my foundation cracks and shifts. BabySitter cannot be my mommy for sure now. She has a daughter, and I'm not her. She can't take two. Her baby will grow up with my favorite life-sized doll that I give them before they leave. That's how much I love them. My face lies. It says I'm happy and excited for a new adventure but my insides are mixed up and not sure what to do. So I keep smiling, hoping Daddy is right about us moving again. Now I pick little red huckleberries that grow out of a tree stump near our gravel driveway. They tickle my tongue and I am happy again. At least for a little while.

✳✳

So far Daddy is right about us moving. Our new family is nice, and I am called Wendy Bill. It's my silly nickname. They teach me to play a card game called Old Maids. I learn the hard way that being dealt the card with the old woman is not good, but I think it is so I hide it and shriek with joy when I'm the one holding her. This teaches me not to cheat and not to cry when I lose a game. But I don't learn to stop being angry for losing. I want to win.

I also learn I cannot speak when sent to school. Something happens and my voice stops working. My shoulders hunch over in hopes of making myself invisible, but I'm too big to hide from myself. Teacher pleads with me to speak. She explains that I must talk at school, so I can learn. She doesn't understand that I don't want to be here. My silence is not enough for her. I sit on the gray concrete outside with my back against the cold brick wall and watch kids play at recess. I refuse to join in. They are not my friends. Best-Friend lives far away. No one else is my friend.

Since my throat won't speak at school, I am sent to another school where we wear white button-up shirts and plaid skirts. This place is nice but we must pray before class. I am one of three tall thin girls. Teacher measures us to see who is tallest. I rejoice that I am the shortest. The other girls like being taller than me, and I am glad for them. They do not understand that I dream of being smaller like Daddy and Grandma. Something inside me wants to hide when I am told that I am tall. Mostly because the tone says there is something wrong with this. It somehow makes me ugly.

**

Daddy is sick and stuck in his room. I visit him and play quietly on the floor, flipping through his music albums, pausing to examine each cover. I like the singer called Tom Jones. His hair is nice and dark like Daddy's. Someone said Daddy's room smells of death. What does death smell like? My nose doesn't understand this. Whispers tell me I could end up without a daddy. What would that mean for me? Who would love me then? A part of me is sad but other parts say not to worry and let the grownups figure this out.

Daddy lives and I go on playing. School ends and we move again. I live with relatives this time. Aunt and Uncle take me in. Cousins and I play and have fun but I must go back to school a bit longer in the same grade I just left until summer. Daddy lives someplace else but I don't know where. He visits sometimes and I'm always excited to see him. We ride up and down the busy street called Capitol Boulevard in our silver blue with white top 1958 Chevy Impala that has a long bench seat up front. I make up a game that we play as we drive.

I tell Daddy that I will hop in the back seat and look for pretty women. When I find one, I'll duck down behind the seat out of view. He is to pull over and talk to her. If she is nice, that will be my signal to pop out of my clever hiding space in the back and ask her if she will be my mommy. Daddy laughs at my idea, but he likes it. We don't find any pretty women to pull over for. We will have to play again another day. I dream of a mommy who smiles when she sees me, who thinks I'm clever, and smart and pretty even when I'm not. I want her to be like Grandma. How could she not be?

**

At last! Daddy finds a mommy for me. Yippee!! Now I get to be like other seven-year-olds! I get to meet her soon. Daddy is excited about her even though I didn't get to help him pick her out. I'll find out more about her soon and the wedding is only about a month away. Oh, yes, at last, my biggest dream is about to come true. I'm about to get a new mommy!

Chapter 3

BAIT AND SWITCH

The handle bars shake and a lump of panic clogs my insides. Tiny bits of gravel fly out from below the bike tires and splash out onto the black paved road. My skinny arms and quivering fingers can no longer control the bike. I'm flying down the hill too fast and I forget how to stop. I freeze but hold on as hard as my muscles will let me. Wobble, wobble slide. Splat! The right side of my body and my head smacks the ground with a thud. Crack. Lights out. My eyes fight to open and I see Aunt standing over me, screaming. She thinks I'm dead. Blood on the road. I close my eyes again and fade into nothing.

Bumps and voices. My head swishes around inside. A man looks at me and tells me something but I don't remember what. He is taking me someplace. Siren shouts that we're passing through. Get out of the way. Back to nothingness.

Something digs flesh from the right side of my head. Screams of my voice wake me to attention and grasp for understanding. Tears do not stop the searing pain. Fire. Fire on my head. Stop! Make it stop! Doctor says he has to make the pain, so I get better. I do not care about that. Just make the torture stop. My head spins, and I give up to the darkness again.

"Where am I?" I cry inside. Where is Daddy? Panic sets in when I see he is gone. I'm trapped in a room all alone. Cries swell in my chest and release uncontrollably out loud. Daddy left me all alone. The room spins and my stomach warns that it might throw up. A nurse comes in and offers me a toy in hopes of hushing the noise. She is impatient with me. I know her tone, because I've heard it before from others. She tells me Daddy isn't here when I ask her for him. I do not know if he will come back for me. I want to go home, but am told I must stay for a few days. I give up, curl up on my bed and whimper myself to sleep.

**

She likes me. The pretty lady's blond hair flips up at the ends like half circles on her shoulders. I want beautiful hair like hers. She runs her hands under the water to make sure it's not too hot. She washes the blood and clumps from my tangled hair that remained after falling off the bike. She doesn't understand how the hospital could have left me like this, but they did. My hair is clean now. I like her.

She works at a bank and went to college. This means she is smart and has lots of money. We talk and smile and she listens to me. She helps me pop blisters that form on the palms of my hands from swinging too much on the monkey bars. She is 19 years-old. I am seven. Daddy is much older than all of us. The wedding is next month and I will be her flower girl. Yes, I like this lady who will be my new mommy.

**

StepGrandma and StepGrandad's house is big and in the middle of a farm. Their bedroom is just off from the front door. StepMom is ordering me into the room. Dim lights cast a glow against the tinted walls. StepMom's angry voice asks me a question that I do not want to answer. She raises her voice and says I must confess. If I speak the truth I will be in trouble, so a lie slips from my tongue. Angry eyes beat into mine. In an instant, she raises a hand and the back side slaps across my face. Whack! Another one. She is holding my right arm, so I can't run away. I must stay in place and accept my punishment. It's what I deserve. Pain throbs in my face and I cannot hold the tears.

Another strike against my head and something catches in the corner of my eye. I cry out extra loud. She suddenly stops whipping my face back and forth, and I have an instant to rush my hand up to my eye. Her wedding ring. That's what got me.

In comes StepGrandma and examines my eye. Her terse lips and angry eyes cut my insides. The wound is invisible but the pain to my flesh, heart and soul freeze in time. How could this be happening? They say that I will be okay and StepMom is sorry, but her anger and my getting hit is my fault. I shouldn't lie. StepGrandma agrees. They wait for me to settle down, control my tears, and we leave the room. I hate them…I hate them both.

StepMom gets angry at me and Daddy nearly every day. But Daddy doesn't get spanked or slapped or his hair pulled. Just me. She doesn't yank on his ears either. Only mine. She says I am spoiled. She scolds me when I don't like her cooking. I try to be good. But I'm not. I'm a bad girl like she says. Good girls don't lie. Good girls act proper. Good girls do as they are told. Good daughters love their mother's cooking. StepMom reminds me of this often. I must love these new people. They are my family now. Oh, this is not the mommy I dreamed of. This one is a monster.

**

Why can't I learn to be a good girl? That is the question StepMom demands that I answer. She is so angry and asks why I can't be more like my new cousins, who she insists are nice and sweet and don't cause her any trouble like I do. I say I try to be good but, as she reminds me yet again, my actions speak louder than words. I am failing at being a good little soldier carrying out orders with precision and speed.

I yearn to be an eagle instead of a little girl and I pretend to fly inside my mind. When I'm not flying, I run as fast as a Cheetah or a speedy brown horse. Run to save myself. Run and hide far, far away. Instead, invisible chains yank me back to this place where I am enslaved and forced to live.

"Be still! Stop fidgeting!" she says but she won't listen when I cry out, telling her that she is brushing my hair too hard and pulling on the strands of my tender scalp. Whack, whack. Whack. Broken hair brushes across the top of my head. Plastic handled brushes are no match for my tough head. The pain vibrates through my body, sending signals to hide. To run. To cry. But I'm not supposed to cry. According to her, being hit doesn't hurt enough to fuss over. She likes to threaten to give me something to *really* cry about. How much pain does it take to have a reason to cry?

**

Daddy shows me little black and white pictures. One of a little boy. The other of a little girl. I marvel at their sweet, friendly faces and look at their pictures as long as I can. He tells me the kids are my big sister and brother. He tells me they live far away in a place called Australia. I don't know where that is, and I don't care. What I care about is seeing and hearing that I have a sister and a brother. He says the photos are old and that they are bigger kids now.

I dream of meeting them one day and us being best friends. But I also wonder what if they don't like me. If they liked me, why did I leave them in the first place? Daddy tells me that my sister and brother don't know about me. That means I'm a secret.

He told me before that I am adopted. Only me. Not Sister or Brother. He says I am his daughter but have another mother and father. This is confusing even though I've heard the news before. I ask him how much he paid for me. I imagine him handing over stacks of money for me, because I must have been expensive. He chuckles and says he didn't pay anything for me.

"Why?" I wonder. Everything costs money. Candy costs money. Clothes cost money. Why not me? Does this mean I am not worth anything? This does not make any sense. You don't just get a daughter for free. Do you? Would a son cost a lot of money? I know Daddy wants a boy. He says so often. Hearing him say this over and over and over makes me wish I was a boy. He would love me more. He would take me to work with him so I wouldn't be alone with StepMom all day.

I don't tell him what StepMom does to me day after day. Or that she doesn't like me all that much. He must already know I am a naughty girl. I don't like this feeling, but can't seem to change it. Daddy has a lot of troubles and I don't like being a pain for him. I don't like seeing StepMom scold him too. I will protect him from my bad behavior, and let him think I am good even on days I'm not. So long as Daddy doesn't know how naughty I really am, then I won't be sold again.

Daddy tells me that as a baby, a family member prophesized that one day I would "return to my people for a season." He tells me that this means that one day I will meet my birth family and stay with them for a while. Hmmm…Could this be true?

**

I have a dream…

I find a young boy lying out in the field of Scotch Broom across from our trailer. The yellow flowering plants cover the ground for nearly as far as my eyes can see. He is about my age with the same color brown hair as me. He is maybe a little bit bigger in size than me. His insides are ripped from his belly and litter the ground. His heart carelessly tossed over here, some squiggly parts over there.

A big hole is where his guts used to be but now the space is empty and bloody. I must save him! He cannot die! I magically find strips of cloth and wrap them around his empty cavern. He is light as I pick him up and hold him gently in my arms. Hurry, I tell myself, we must find help.

Off we fly, searching the ground from above for someone to help us. We fly to the trailer next door to where I live but no one there can help. A voice from somewhere tells me I have to heal him myself. I don't know how to heal. I am not a doctor. I have magic powers to fly but that is all I know. Frantic! He will die soon. I MUST save this beautiful young boy. Both of our lives depend on me and my magic right now.

I wake up panicked about the boy. Images of his empty, bloody shell lingers in my brain all day like a ghost. I dream about him with my eyes open and pretend I do save him and he loves me for it. I pretend he is my friend or my brother and I am the hero who heals him. I like this boy. If only he was for real.

**

Daddy is told not to let me be alone with Cousin1 because he is a bad boy and can't be trusted around girls. We are visiting family out of state and I am the only girl old enough to go outside and play with the boys. Daddy talks with the grownups and says it's okay if I go for a walk with Cousin1 since Cousin2 will be with me.

We three walk down the block. Cousin1 stands several feet taller than my 8-year-old self. He is big and twice my age. I do not know him well and mostly stay silent as he banters with Cousin2. Me in the middle. From the outside, we look like two big boys walking and protecting a little girl from traffic or any other threat.

Cousin1 changes his tone and a devilish grin crosses his face. His energy shifts from friendly to pending trouble. He grabs hold of my left arm and tells Cousin2 that it's a good idea to rape me. I do not understand this word. I look up and see glee in Cousin1's eyes and realize that rape must be something bad. Cousin2 says no, it's not a good idea because I am just a little girl.

Their voices slice my chest and I feel my insides clamp up like a giant ball of steel. I need to run, but I am held against my will by a big hand that still holds a tight grip on my left arm. Cousin1 pulls me forward against my will and shows us thick bushes he says will be a great spot to assault me. He practically drags me there and I am unable to stop him. He is so much stronger than me and determined to have his way. The bushes are closer now and something inside me screams that if I go to the bushes, I won't live to tell about it.

This has to stop! How? Cousin1 is even more determined now than ever to hide me in the bushes and infect me with his twisted cheap thrill. He is like a hunter killing an animal for sport and tossing out the carcass. He insists it will be fun. How can this act called rape be fun when the word alone overflows my body with terror? I some-how know that rape will destroy me before it kills me. No! I scream inside. NO! NO! NO! He must NOT get his way. I have heard the adults say he is spoiled and used to getting his way. StepMom says

I am spoiled, but I am not spoiled enough to hurt anyone. I am not evil spoiled. I do things that are naughty but deep down I am a good girl.

Cousin2 refuses to be a part of something so sick and *wrong*. He grabs my right arm in an effort to free me and I am now pulled between boys. My insides are choking, and I don't know what to do but cry and do my best to stop Cousin1 from pulling on me anymore. "Please don't hurt me," I silently plead. My mind lurches forward in time and I see myself lying on the ground, fighting for my life. Screaming into the wind and kicking with all my might.

Even though I don't know rape for real, this is the image that flashes before the eyes inside my mind. My body says Cousin1 will hurt me more than a spanking or slaps across the face. Fear, mixed with hatred and rage begin to surge through my veins. Not only for Cousin1 and his evil plan but also for Daddy for letting me go outside with this beast.

Cousin1's father is known as a God-fearing man. He preaches how people are sinners and need to repent. Does he not know that Satan lives with him and he calls him Son? Cousin1 did not learn the lesson of being good. I do not believe his father is the perfect man he thinks he is either to have a son like this.

Cousins stop pulling on my arms and Cousin1 decides to save the rape for another time. He threatens me that I must promise not to ever tell. "I promise," I whisper. I somehow know if I tell, he will destroy me. Our secret, mixed with even more hatred and terror buries itself deep within my bones.

We casually walk through the doorway to the house. Daddy and others are still yakking up a storm and don't notice our arrival at first. I slink into the bathroom and lower the toilet seat and sit.

StepMom comes in and sees me sitting, in silence, frozen. She asks me what is wrong. I worry that my face tells secrets that I promised to bury forever. My voice refuses to speak. I gaze straight ahead towards the wall, keeping eyes off StepMom.

She asks me again what happened. Her voice tells me it's okay to spill what's lingering just inside my chest. She is smart. But not wise enough to understand that I promised not to tell the wickedness that I narrowly escaped. She is the only one who notices that my body has a story to tell. I cannot even tell her how Cousin2 saved me from horror that no one should endure. I cannot tell her Cousin2 is my hero. He will not get any praise or medals for his bravery. Only satisfaction that he is not a devil too.

I do not understand why, but even though Daddy threw me out with that creature, I am the one who needs to protect Daddy. He would feel bad if he know Cousin1 threatened to rape me. At least I think he would. It is my job to protect Daddy. He suffers enough.

No, Cousin1 doesn't have to worry. I hate him. Will hate and fear him forever, but will never tell a soul what happened. I'll swallow today and bury it in a vault.

**

I hide under the neighbors' bushes in their front yard, safely out of sight from passing cars. Night fell hours ago, and I choose to stay outside, playing with imaginary villains. Mysterious people drive by, car after car, their headlights missing my clever hiding space. They are the enemy that I hide from to survive. Where are they going? Where do they live? I will never know and really don't care. The story I create in my mind is far cleverer than reality.

Warm night air kisses my skin and brings peace. Being alone, outside in my own little world is how I like to spend time. It's better than being stuck inside where the walls and rules confine me and I have to stay on alert to sudden attacks from StepMom. A covered light bulb exposes our front porch but I'm not home and the light's reach is too short to find me next door. Yes, I am well hidden. And safe. For now.

StepMom's voice cracks the stillness of my imaginary space and time. Her cranky cat call, "WENDY!" threatens to end my solitude but I do not wish to be disturbed. Shhh, I tell myself. Don't answer. Stay quiet and stay outside a little longer. I'm not tired and I don't want to go to bed. I'm having fun and not ready to give up my secret spot.

Again, her voice cuts through the once calm night, "WEEEEN-DYYYYY!" Still, I refuse to respond. After a few more outbursts, with the octave and intensity of her voice screeching and roaring like an angry bear, I finally give in and responded.

"What?"

That was it. That's all it took. I sold myself out and now the game is over.

"It's after dark! Get home NOW!" she growls. Her tone tells me to move quickly and don't stop in front of her. I must scurry to my bedroom as soon as I pass through the front doorway. She likes to yank the tiny hairs at the nape of my neck until I cry out so I must not let that happen. If she can't grab my hair, she goes straight for an ear.

Reluctantly, and with a game plan for my fast escape, I crawl out from under the bush and scoot the few yards home. Her words cut the air like an angry butcher with a big knife. She scolds me the whole way spewing how angry and disappointed she is and calling me names for ignoring her. How *dare* I ignore her majesty? She orders me to get ready for bed. Pronto.

She storms through the house after me, raised voice cutting my chest and belly. I aim towards the bathroom before my bedroom. She informs me that she is not done with me yet. And she speaks the truth.

Out of nowhere the back of her bony hand bashes against my face. The force of her wrath snaps my head to the side like a broken doll. Angry hand connects with my nose. Blood. Sprays of blood splattering on the white porcelain sink. Blood flying across the room landing on the walls. Purple flowered wallpaper now tainted with spots of red. All I see is red, white, and blurs of purple. My face cries out for her to stop. My nose gushing blood eager to escape. I fight to stay standing and not topple over by the force of her blows. She holds my left arm so I cannot escape. "I'm sorry!" I cry. But she doesn't want to hear it. She doesn't believe me and sneers that actions speak louder than words.

Her eyes burn hatred and disgust for me deep inside my soul. Her eyes speak more than her words or the physical pain. She does not hide the fact that she loathes me when I disappoint her. She warns that she plans to teach me a lesson. And she does. She teaches me to hate her even more than I already do. But I cannot allow myself to feel this because it's not allowed. I am only to express love and happiness.

She finishes her flogging and spewing of rage. I do my best to clean up the liquid mess that is mine. Swallow the hatred for her that grows in my belly, bigger than a watermelon. Temper down the urge to lash out and kill her. It's my fault. I created this blood bath. Satisfaction slides off her lips as she gives me permission to now tell all my friends that I was beaten. No, this is another secret I will harbor in the ever growing chamber of doom. My friends do not need to know what a naughty girl I am. Something shifts inside me and I know that I will never be the same.

Building, building, building an invisible wall. Stuffing life into the deepest, darkest crevices of my gut. StepMom loves telling me not to cry or else she'll "give me something to cry about." What wretched rules that beatings and spankings and hair pulling are not reasons to cry. What is a good enough reason to wail? Stuff, stuff, stuff. "Stop crying, Wendy," I secretly say to myself. "You don't want more of the same so keep quiet. Be strong. Don't let her know what she's really doing to you."

StepMom reminds me often that when we are good, God loves us. He gets angry and vengeful when we are bad. She is simply like God. When I am good, she loves me. When I am bad, I suffer in hell. Hell must be where I'm going since I am so naughty.

I don't like Hell. It's full of fire and I will burn to death only I won't die. Sinners never die. They just burn forever in their own special lake. Sinners can't drown either. They can only fry. Please, God. I am sorry. Please don't make me burn in Hell. I promise to be a better girl tomorrow.

I will work harder in school. Do better at math. Stop writing so hard that I cannot erase my mistakes without ripping holes in the paper. StepMom threatens to make me wear short dresses to school so my classmates and teacher can see the bruises on my upper legs. That way I will be ashamed of myself and work even harder at being good.

I accidentally break drinking glasses while washing the dishes, causing StepMom to shriek and shame me to be careful and not be so stupid. I don't mean to. I promise. I know I do a bad job vacuuming and miss the little pieces of lint that sticks to the clingy fibers of the carpet. I neglect to pull back throw rugs and clean under them too. StepMom notices little details that I miss. Her sharp tongue lashes me for my laziness.

She scolds me for not eating all of my food. She knows I hate her mushy peas that pop out of their skin but she makes me eat every green ball on my plate. I'm not allowed to vomit them up. Or hide them. She lets me drown them in catchup and salt and pepper but even that does not hide the disgust. She also refuses to listen that I cannot eat as much as she insists is the right amount. I am always the last one to leave the table. My stomach fights to choke down more bites. She tells me I am ungrateful for there are starving kids in China who would love to have my food. I would send them what is on my plate if I could but I don't know where China is.

I ache to be with Grandma. She lives down a few streets and I visit her when I can. The long walk through the cemetery that takes me to the busy street to her place is a treat I am allowed from time to time. StepMom doesn't like me visiting Grandma too much because she says I come back spoiled, and she has to retrain me. I feel safe with Grandma and wish I could live with her but I can't. Grandma is too sick to take care of anyone for long. She is still sick from when I was four.

Oh, dear God. Why can't I follow directions like I'm told the first time? I write a song and sing out loud in the safety of my bedroom. My song tells God that I am ready to die. I promise I will be good so I can go to Heaven. I just want out of here. I welcome death any time.

Grownups in my family sit around and talk about God and how all those of us who are good and worthy in God's eyes will be saved. Jesus is coming any time now to whisk us up and away. All the bad people will stay behind and die. We are special because we believe the Truth. One Truth is that we must never end our life early or else we will surely perish and become a child of the Devil. This tells me that even though I welcome death, I must suffer alive for as long as God intends. No options of an early exit by my own hands. The fear of the alternative keeps me alive.

Chapter 4

MR. AND MRS. GOD

I like 5th grade so far. Halloween is weeks away but that doesn't really matter. Pagan Trick-or-Treating is not allowed. Good Christians don't go around house to house begging for candy. Plus it's tainted with razors and drugs that will make a kid go crazy. I remember the thrill of bringing home a pillow case with lots of candy as a kid before StepMom came along but that was a long time ago.

Dad calls me out to the garage. He spends a lot of time here tinkering around and now he wants to talk to me about something. He is serious and I'm not sure if I'm in trouble as always. A little knot forms in my belly and I slink towards him, bracing for the worst. His tone shifts and becomes less stern. I'm not in trouble! He asks me if I would like to live on a farm for a while. He isn't sure how long. "YES!" I answer. Oh, what an unexpected turn of luck! Together we paint pictures in our minds of me actually living in the country. Wide open fields to run and jump in. Milking cows like a real farmer. Oh, what a dream come true!

My plastic horse collection will now be replaced with a REAL horse. My mind pretends that me and my brown horse with her black mane and tail ride against the wind in wide open fields. I see myself with my legs snuggly wrapped around her furry belly and me holding onto leather reigns. We move in unison as we gallop until the land ends.

Dad says I can live that dream very soon. Oh, how did I get so lucky? He reminds me of people who we used to know when I was younger. I remember liking them. He tells me they moved to another state and own a big farm there and I get to go live with them.

He shows me two new suitcases that he bought just for me. One is bigger than the other. Green tapestry flowers adorn the outside. What special gifts they are. They will hold my clothes while I fly on a big airplane. He tells me I will be flying with a lady friend. She and I fly from Seattle to some place far away. I don't know where this is and I don't care. All I care about is having my own horse on a farm. Life is good.

I say goodbye to my family and board the giant plane. On the ride over, the lady I travel with says we are going to a wedding. Her son is getting married on the farm that will be my new home. Weddings are fun. I like the lady I travel with. We met before. She is nice to me and smiles a lot. I am happy that we are together.

**

Our airplane lands and my dream life is only a car ride away now. Butterflies fill my stomach and I embrace my good luck. MrGod and MrsGod greet us and we fill them in on our long journey. They pack my old life that is inside my suitcases in the trunk. We drive forever south to a place outside of a small town. I still don't understand where I am. What I do know is that I am a long way from home. And my dream is now real.

We turn left off the main highway and slowly drive up a long dirt road. Trees and a bit of field spread outside the window. We stop not far from a small tattered house, a nice double-wide trailer house and other single-wide trailer houses that are not as new. Big barns and another building dot the property. A wire fence shows animals are not free to wander around the homes.

Lots of people I don't know greet us. They tell me that everyone lives here together on TheFarm. I'm not sure if I like this old, dirty place or not. The space between me and home is far. Is it too far? I assure myself that this will be all that I dreamed. Dad forgot to tell me that I'd miss him and Grandma. Well, after the wedding, I can go home. Where are the cows and horses?

The wedding is more than one. I remember Dad and StepMom's wedding. I wore my lavender flower girl dress and walked down the aisle. I remember painting Dad's car for celebration and green paint stained my dress. At their wedding, they were the only ones in front of the minister saying, "I do." But here, there are three brides and three grooms. They repeat their vows together as the rest of our group stands around watching. MrGod is in charge of the ceremony. I do not understand why so many people are getting married at one time. But I do not focus on that question for long. I am sad to discover that Dad was wrong. This farm doesn't have a horse for me. Or anyone else. No need to stay here then. I'll leave really soon and see Dad and Grandma again before I know it.

I sleep in a bedroom in an old small house that sits on a hill away from everyone else. Princess and I share the three bedroom house with another lady who comes and goes but pays little attention to us. We must use a rickety outhouse and cannot wash our hands afterwards. This scares me every time because I worry that a snake is curled up under the makeshift toilet and will bite me on my butt. Only the trailer houses have toilets that flush.

We all eat three hot meals together every day in the first house I saw on arrival. Boys sleep in the bedroom on bunks. Women stir, and cook and wash dishes in the kitchen. A menu for the month is posted on the wall so we know to alert our stomachs each day. We pray in the living room many times every day. People cry and speak in a language I've never understood but heard before. Mrs-God shakes and slaps her tambourine against the palm of her hand, singing songs to God and Jesus. MrGod tells us stories reminding us to be good or else God will punish us.

This place is not my home. I am more than ready to fly back to my old life and see Grandma and Dad. The lady I flew with is leaving and I think I am leaving with her. But no…MrGod and MrsGod take me into the living room where we meet for prayer. MrsGod looks in my eyes and tells me I am home. This is my new home. They tell me I will go to school here.

Her words, even though meant to be soft and soothing, pull a trigger. Something inside me explodes. All time stands still and breath catches in my lungs. For an instant, I freeze. A death-like wail cries out from my soul. My body shakes as I insist between sobs that I must go home. I need Dad and Grandma. MrGod and MrsGod struggle to make me stop crying. Nothing works. Their earnest prayers to God do not even begin to heal the raw, bloody wound that consumes me. My insides crumble and I wish I could disappear.

The truth hits me that Dad was wrong about so many things. There is no horse. He said I'd only be here for a short time. I feel… betrayed. He did not tell me I would never see him or Grandma again. I turn off my ears to the words of MrGod and MrsGod and cave in. This is where I live now. My old home is too far to run to. I'm no longer wanted there anyway.

**

All eyes stare at me as I walk through the door to my new class-room. Teacher asks me what I learned at my other school. My mind is blank and only whispers come out of my mouth. She gives me a test to see how many states and capitals I know. Not many. She is worried if I know much at all. She is nice to me even though I might not be too smart. Kids are nice to me too.

We jump rope at recess. I am a master at jumping rope and one of the longest jumpers. This makes my insides smile as well as my face. Around and around the rope goes, slapping the ground. My feet jump just high enough to miss the rope as it passes under me. Double jump with only me in the middle. Double jump with someone else. It's usually not me who misses the step and falters. I don't mind that someone else is not as good of a jumper as me. They will learn if they focus hard like I do.

One of the men on TheFarm, Savior, lets me help him feed the cows while he milks them. He is nice to me and likes when I hang out with him. He lets me watch as a calf is born. The mother lies on her side and moans and wiggles as best she can. Savior says her calf is stuck. He slips his hands inside the mother cow and grabs hold of the calf's legs. He pulls and pulls and pulls hard. A beautiful, wet and slimy calf slides out. She is perfect and we celebrate that the mother will be okay. I like being with Savior. He listens to me talk and talk and talk. He lets me be grown up and pour molasses on the dry feed for the cows to eat. The brown gooey syrup coats the kernels making our milk sweeter when it comes out.

Rabbits, rabbits, so many rabbits. I do not understand why we have so many rabbits. And geese. I do not like geese and they do not like me. A baby goose is injured and needs extra love. I take the baby goose and make it my own. I find scrap wood and cloth material and make it a bed. Baby goose likes me but I know it won't for long. Geese bite and chase and this one will one day too so I don't keep it to myself for long.

Winter is snowy and icy. Princess and I help make special shoes that tie on to the bottom of our regular shoes. The special shoes have nails in them to cut into the ice as we climb the hill to our tiny house where we sleep. We slip and slide and laugh off our shivers from the cold.

Christmas comes and Princess is the only who gets presents. Dad calls me on the phone and tells me it would not be fair if he sent me a gift and not one for everyone else. He doesn't understand that Princess got a special jewelry box for Christmas. Dad's call is my only gift. He wrote me a couple short letters which tells me that he remembers me sometimes.

Princess keeps me on guard. Some days she is happy and we play together. Some days she'd rather I be gone from here and I don't blame her. I wish to be gone too. Sadness fills my heart over missing my old home that I will never see again. This is Princess's home and she doesn't like sharing all the time. She likes trouble though but I don't. She lies and steals and puts stuff in my pockets when we are in stores. I tell her not to do this but she flashes me her warning look that says she will hurt me if I refuse. So I do as she says. Physical pain is something I do not miss from my old home and Princess threatens me with it.

Princess gets a Shetland pony named Cinnamon! Rejoice! At last TheFarm has a horse. I am allowed to ride Cinnamon too. We take turns galloping her as fast as she will go. I fall off her slippery bare back over and over and over but I do not care. Breath escapes me or gets caught inside my chest after each fall. I rest until I can settle down and regain proper breathing again. But I do not care how many times this happens. I climb on Cinnamon's back and keep riding. I am free with the wind in my hair and my legs around Cinnamon's stout body. This is my dream come true.

**

Snakes. Snakes on the road. Prince dangles a fat dead rattle snake in my face and laughs as I panic and instinctually recoil for safety. He threatens to throw the nightmare on me and tells me it's really alive. I know that if a snake bites, you die. I do not want to die the slow death of venom flowing through my veins. I am weary from being the target of Prince and Princess. Their glee is always at my expense.

Princess laughs as she forces me to place my neck in a noose that she and another girl tie to the swing set. She finds humor in the thought of my dead torso dangling from the rope around my neck. She assures me that she won't let me really die but oh what fun she will have watching me beg her for life. Savior sees what she is doing and orders her to stop. She does but her brain still ticks and plots ways to embed fear and submission into me.

She coerces me into the barn, up on bales of hay. She ties my arms and legs to hooks on the wall so I cannot run. She says I am bad and must be punished. She says I better pray snakes don't come get me. If they do, I will die. She laughs an evil tone while I struggle to set myself free. I hate her, fear her, pity her and for some unexplainable reason, love her and want her to love me too.

 Her brown eyes and pretty face defy what she really is. She is poison on the inside. There is nothing I can do about this either. She is the Princess and I must obey her. MrGod and MrsGod do not believe me when I tell them how she really is. They believe instead that I am the one who misbehaves.

I open the door to our three-roomed house and Princess jumps out from hiding, tackles me and pounds a shoe with a wooden heal into my thigh. Whack, whack, whack. She laughs and tells me I deserve what I get. Searing pain jolts down my legs and my insides shrivel up even more and more. I do not understand why God created me. Life tells me over and over than I am the biggest mistake He ever made. I know I must die. I must die and pay for being born. I ask Princess to kill me since I am such a naughty girl. A waste. She refuses my plea which confuses me even more.

**

People think I am happy here. My outside lies as I bury the truth deep inside my secret catacomb of memories. No one must see the emptiness inside. I am alone and walking down the hill from where I sleep. Giant black ants cross the gravelly road. I've seen these ants before and I don't like them. I find matches. Strike one of the wooden matches and watch the flame jump out. I squish and murder an ant with fire and relish in its painful death as it squirms for freedom. Mercy is not an option.

Killing the ant gives me a moment of release from the pressure that is built up inside my chest. But now, my heart is whispering that it was wrong to kill an innocent creature. My insides soften and I offer a belated, "I'm so sorry," to the dead ant. "I didn't mean to hurt you." Guilty tears flood me and I promise to never hurt anything again.

**

Me and Princess ride Cinnamon off of the property, cross the busy road and visit a neighbor boy. Princess likes to visit here often but I don't. NeighborBoy who lives here is 16 years-old. He meets us outside and is happy to see us. Princess lets me sit on Cinnamon while the three of us talk. NeighborBoy leans his lanky body up close to me and slides his hand to where my private parts are. He smiles real big and Princess asks me if I like him doing that. My insides freeze and a scream sticks in my throat. No! I do NOT like this! Why would I like NeighborBoy touching my dirty private parts? StepMom told me over and over and over how dirty the hidden area is between my legs. She said it is the germiest part of my body. Worse than my dirty feet after playing barefoot outside.

NeighborBoy reminds me of Cousin1. A similar sinister smirk crosses his face. He pretends that I really do like him touching me so he wants to do it again. I need to run away on Cinnamon's back but I am trapped again. Princess sees my frozen body and even though she thinks it is funny, she agrees that NeighborBoy can touch me again another time. She talks to me about having sex with boys and says it's fun. I do not understand sex but the tone and the vibration that pounds though my young body tells me that sex is not right for me. Boys and sex are something I must protect myself from. I will refuse to ever visit here again.

**

I like wandering through the trees that surround our vast property. Curiosity often leads me down paths that I'd otherwise not explore. Being in the trees makes me feel safe and I remember the ones I climbed at my old home where I lived with Dad. Today is a special day for a walk through the woods though. Today is the day I am going to die.

My plan is brilliant. All I have to do is wander into the thickness, get lost and never be found. No one will miss me and if they do they will be glad I'm gone. Naughty children are not liked and I am not liked here except by a few. Not like I was in the beginning when everyone welcomed me with open arms and excitement of a new member of the group.

I am tired of my growing body going to bed hungry some nights. I am weary from praying in the living room every day while MrGod tells us what we are doing wrong and the punishments we will endure if we do not save ourselves from sin. There is no reason for me to live any longer. I ask God to let me die today. He is smart enough to help me lose my way and never be found. Yes, this is a good plan. Everything will be over soon.

I wander left and right, deeper into the trees. I am ready to surrender to death at any moment. My feet take off on their own, leading me around familiar ground. I look up to the tops of the trees and notice how small I am compared to them. Dusk is setting. It won't be much longer now until I'm well and truly lost forever. A peace and mild excitement, a relief, really, engulfs me.

Step, step, step. I look up from the ground, expecting to see a new place in the woods. Eager to find and soak in the spot where I'll say good-by to the world. What?! My feet defy me! They lead me back to where I started. A sigh slips my lips. I cannot believe that I cannot even die right! Why, God, didn't you let me get lost and die today? My heart sinks. I take myself back to the others and resign myself to the fact that I'll continue living here…for a very long time.

**

I resist Princess's idea but she continues to wear me down. My body screams NO! as I finally, reluctantly surrender myself to her demands. She says it's time to get me "ready for boys". I lie across the bed like a whimpering dog with my belly exposed, unsure what to expect next. My pants are pulled down over my feet and tossed aside. My underpants slide off over my legs and join my pants. Princess gleams at me with her wicked smile, laced with kindness. Her double-edged sword.

Princess tells me it will only hurt for a little while and will be worth it. Boys will like me more this way. I don't care about boys. But I do care about making Princess happy. When she is happy, I can be happy. She tells Helper to hold me down by the arms so I don't move. Princess speaks as if this is my idea but it's too much to process right now so I stop wriggling as she sticks something hard and penetrating up my vagina. Her voice seeks to soothe me as she pushes harder in an effort to tear the protective tissue inside me and make me bleed. Pain seers through my private parts and I fade to numb, assuring myself that this will be over soon.

When she is finished, we go on about the night as if nothing out of the ordinary happened. But I know deep down that a part of me will never be the same. And God knows, I'll never tell anyone. This is our biggest secret yet. With her mission accomplished, Princess is pleased with herself. She says I can be with NeighborBoy now if I want. But I don't want NeighborBoy. Or any other boy. I stifle the burning need to cry. But I must be brave instead.

**

Our garden is big enough to feed all of us. We are many mouths. Some are young children. Others are adults. And some, older like me, Princess and Prince. Today Princess and I pull weeds from the dark soil to make room for vegetables to grow bigger. It's hot and I do not like this work. Princess tells me that she is angry at me. Venom drips from her tongue and I struggle to ignore her, yet listening at the same time.

Word came earlier this morning that I am leaving TheFarm today and I'm not coming back. EarthAngels came to pick me up and drive me to my old home where I lived with Dad. I have not seen EarthAngels yet. They are waiting for me in town at a restaurant. I am told to pack my belongings and be ready for someone to drive me into town and be passed off to my new charges. EarthAngels are not allowed on the property. They must wait for my eventual arrival and passing off of the burden of me…No matter how long it takes to transport me from here to there. Come to think of it, no other outsiders came here either.

Princess barks orders telling me to keep working at pulling weeds until I leave. No break time allowed. She cuts me with her eyes and the sneer on her pursed lips when my name is called to say goodbye. She threatens that if I ever tell anyone what happened to me while living here that she would hunt me down and kill me. I know she is true to her word. Ice forms inside me and I promise never to tell. Before I fully comprehend what is happening, I look back at the dusty road that marks my departure. A right hand turn signals an end to my shattered dream. But my heart grows hopeful as TheFarm fades behind me.

**

Our journey to Washington is comfortable in the motor home. We drive days and nights taking time to swim in a pool. I sit mostly in silence. EarthAngels and their two young daughters are happy to see me every day. They hug me and tell me they are glad I am with them. They tell me I am loved. They ask me if I understand that I am loved. No. I do not understand this.

They wonder if I am eager to see my family again. I do not know. Should I be happy to see someone I have not seen in nine months? I do not know how I feel about returning to a house where I have my own bedroom, running water and a toilet that flushes. How is a child supposed to feel whose dashed dreams turned into a nightmare that must be stuffed to the bottom of her toes, never to be spoken? Tightness and pressure in my chest and belly is what I know for sure. Beyond that, I simply feel… nothing.

My insides stir as we near my old house. My mind races and I ask myself questions faster than I can answer. Will Dad and StepMom want to see me? Or if not, will they send me away again? Am I happy to see them? So many questions freeze in space waiting for answers. But do I really want to know what is about to happen next? Darkness of the night hides me until we pull into the driveway.

The same porch light casts a bright glow on the step that leads to our front door. Dad and StepMom appear and a part of me shrivels up inside, wishing to hide, afraid to show my face. It is too hard to tell if they are really happy I am home or if they are wearing masks. I want to believe their joy but trust is missing from my heart.

Dad stays home from work the next day to be with me. He says he is glad I am with him again and his words feel true. We both struggle to know where to begin talking to each other after nine long, life changing months apart. He makes the bigger effort and smiles when he looks at me.

My stomach growls but I am too afraid to ask for food. I wander around this old house like a new guest from another planet, afraid of touching something that I shouldn't. Dad assures me that I do not have to ask for food. That if I am hungry, I can get myself something to eat. He doesn't understand that I am programmed to ask for everything so this is a new thought process.

At home, there are no church meetings. No prayer meetings. Only three of us sit at the table instead of many. My room is to myself and I have space for my things. So much of what I left behind is still here, waiting for me to rediscover.

I am still confused about how I fit in with life here. I do not fully understand what happened to me while away. It is July and summer is still strong so I do not have to worry about school for a while. This is good because I am not ready to start 6th grade yet. I'm not sure I'm ready for anything really. Adjusting to the change of surroundings and rules is taking time. The inside of my head stays jumbled and my body is on alert for the unknown that could strike out and get me at any time. Is this how life is for everyone else?

Chapter 5

SKELETON EXPOSED

Dreaming is what I do best. In school while others do as Teacher says, I stare out the window and take myself to faraway places. I travel this way often. Away from my reality, I am happy, free and loved. I dream of Mother. In my pretend world, Mother smiles as she lovingly gazes at me. She beams with pride that I am her daughter. We laugh at silly jokes like me and Grandma do. Mother is sorry that she had to give me away for adoption as a baby and never see me again.

In my fantasy, we are together forever and I am the love of her life. She is kind and gentle and never hurts me. She keeps me safe from the harshness of the outside world. These images that float through my head give me reason to smile on the inside. One day I will meet her. It is prophecy. I hang on to Dad's words from my youth that one day I will return to my people for a season. But how much of my dreaming will be accurate and how many details will remain a fantasy?

**

I am still Dad's only son. I am his daughter too but he reminds me

73

and others that he still longs for a boy. That is impossible for him and I feel guilty that I do not fulfill him. He teaches me to cut and stack wood. He guides me as he shows me how to use a hammer to pound in nails. Careful not to whack my fingers or thumb. He taught me early on how to thread wriggly worms on the end of a sharp fishing hook without squealing like a scared little girl. He tells me to watch so I learn how to gut and skin fish that we fry for dinner. I am a better fisherman than Dad. He likes this about me. So do I. Would a son be better at these things than I am?

Dad lets me row our small aluminum boat as we cast our lines and wait for a fish to reel in. When my arms are tired from pushing and pulling the water with the oars, we drop anchor and sit. My line always has a red and white bobber at the end. That way we can see for sure if a fish takes the treat I tempt it with. Dad tells me to sit still and that I am so wiggly. Sitting still is something I cannot seem to do. StepMom always scolds me, telling me to sit still at home too and to stop bouncing my legs. I don't know why but my body must be moving at all times. Even when I sleep. I know this because I wake up with tangled sheets and blankets. And sometimes I'm far from where I started on the mattress.

Being alone with Dad on the water is peaceful. It's a place where we can both let down our guard and laugh. Fishing is something Step-Mom doesn't like to do so we leave her behind. We are glad she is not a fisherman like us. We relish in escaping the negative charged vibration that is our home. Neither of us like it there.

He leaves me as often as possible to drive to work and stays away long days. I do not like being home without him. Even if he has to spank me with a freshly cut switch from one of our trees for being naughty. He loves me and tells me so. He smiles at me from his heart and says that I am clever. This tells me that I am close to being good enough as a daughter. At least on some days.

Our giant walnut tree on the side of the house is my frequent refuge. Strong branches reach out and nearly touch the glass of my bedroom window. My skinny arms and legs skillfully scale the bark as I climb as high as I can reach. I pretend that I can live curled up on a branch. I am a master tree climber. No tree is too high or tricky for me. If only I could hoist myself out my bedroom window onto the savior that is my tree, I could escape the harshness inside the walls undetected.

When Grandma is well enough, we sew clothes for me. We bake raisin pie, rhubarb pie and fried apple pies. She is a master at baking Apple Stack Cake. Only she knows the secret to the moist layers of cake that bathe in homemade apple sauce and stack at least 8" high. Her masterpiece is family tradition. No one makes this like her. She is legendary. Not even I can replicate her expertise. But Grandma worries me because she must take dozens of pills to keep alive.

At school I learn that I am a funny writer. But my handwriting still gets me in trouble. StepMom makes me sit and practice writing, spelling and math after school every day. A teacher said I would not make a good secretary because my penmanship is too poor. This is considered bad but I am happy that I will not grow up sitting behind a desk, taking orders from a man. But this is my secret because I do not want to disappoint anyone any more right now than I already do. Girls are expected to work in an office and do what the boss man says. Not me. I'll be different. But I don't know how just yet.

Crafting and stitching puppets and putting on shows is something I like to do. Pretending to be someone else in another time and space frees me from what I must face when the curtain is lowered on the cardboard stage.

Friends are my refuge too. We play outside until dark, regretting that the day is over. We ride bikes up and down the street, speeding on the sidewalk when we can. We leap over grave sites in the cemetery and make up sad stories about the people buried below our feet. Sometimes we take the dying flowers out of the trash that were discarded by grounds keepers if they have a hint of life left in them.

Air is freeing and I long to be free outside every day. I still dream of my own horse and pretend I am grown up on my own farm. We do not talk about me being away from home for nine months. We do not talk about the fact that TheFarm did not have a horse for me. I do not talk about the horror and torment that rolled around inside me day after day.

Nobody knows that I get scared and do not always want to be alive. These are my secrets that I keep to myself. When they threaten to come out, I stuff them deeper inside me so that not even I dare let myself know how truly tormented I am. It's safer to go on silently believing my life is normal. And keeping the real me hidden…out of sight. Some things just are not to be talked about.

✶✶

My insides buzz around like busy bees in a hive. Little stings of excitement surge through my veins and charge the air with static. She is coming to meet me. Mother! Word is that she is flying to America and plans to see me face to face. This must mean that she thinks of me like I think of her. She must dream of missing her tiny baby that she gave away and wants me back. She must be sorry for our separation…I forgive her. At last I am on the fringes of finally having a mother who loves me. She plans to come along with family members who live in Canada. They will all come see me. I love this family in Canada and am eager to see them again.

LittleBrother is coming too. News of his birth a few years ago reached me and gouged my heart. My space in the family was filled by another baby. A boy. This one did not have to find a new home. Why did I? What makes this little boy more special than I am? I do my best to understand why Sister and Brother are better than me, but why this one who replaced me? These questions niggle in the back of my mind from time to time and now they are in the forefront praying for answers.

The phone rings a loud shrill from its hanging spot on the wall between the kitchen and living room. StepMom answers and her tone is serious towards someone on the other end. She gets a little angry at this person as they exchange words that I do not fully hear. She hangs up and needs to tell me something.

She tells me Mother is coming but she, StepMom is not happy about this. She claims I am HER daughter. She does not want me hurt by this woman who gave birth to me. She says Mother had her chance to have me but she gave me up. This is true but I must meet my real mother. Hearing StepMom say that I am hers confuses me yet gives me a glimmer of hope that she really might love me after all. Seeing her as a good mother bear is new to me. How do I handle the dueling for my affection?

On some level I do believe that StepMom loves me but she can never fill the vast emptiness of my hollowed out soul that longs to be filled with a mother's unconditional love. In my mind, life would be perfect being with Mother. No one understands how my heart longs to be loved by the mother who created me. Who carried me around in the safety of her womb and pushed me out into this world. No one understands that even though we do not know each other, there are invisible cords that connect us that cannot be removed. These are all feelings that I must keep inside me. If they escape, then someone will get hurt. I must protect the adults in my life. Making life easier for them is my job. One day they may love me for it.

My room must be tidied up and ready for Mother to sleep here. Bed made. Clothes and toys put away. I wind up my clock to make sure Mother always knows what time it is. This is important. Keeping track of time is critical to being on time getting up, going to bed and going to school. The rapid ticking of the clock sounds like the inside of my heart.

Mother arrives. She enters our small house through the back door that is used as the main entrance. It is obvious that I will grow to be much taller than she is. Her face is soft and her blondish-brown hair curls. Not like my straight, stringy hair. LittleBrother follows behind her. He is not as shy as Mother or I. We hug but I'm unable to fully absorb its meaning. The meeting of my dreams is almost too much to absorb. Part of me is eager to please her and prove to her that I am lovable. Other parts of me say to be silent. Do not let on to the troublemaker that I am.

A silent static in the air clears and everyone sits and looks at each other, making small talk. LittleBrother whines and acts out. I am not sure about having a little brother. He already seems like a spoiled brat. If he lived in my home, surely he would be spanked regularly like me for he seems even naughtier. He knows me as Cousin Wendy in America. Not as his big sister.

I show Mother my room and we are alone for a few minutes. We struggle to find words and push them out of our mouths. She smiles but her smile holds back something. She does not like my clock so I must remove it. I thought for sure she would like this clock. What else about me will she not like?

Mother does not apologize for making me live in America while the rest of them sailed away to another country. She does not tell me she is proud of me. She does not really say much to me but she is happy to be here. So many unspoken words and feelings get discarded as the time ticks by. What I do hear though is that I am a family secret. I am the skeleton in the closet that is rattling and on the verge of exposure. Mother is told in no uncertain terms that Sister and Brother must know about me. Father must be willing to admit that I exist and am alive. Being a secret burns and shames me. I do not like being known as Cousin Wendy in America. I know that my flesh is more than that.

We drive to Canada with family. StepMom and Dad stay in Washington. This is a special trip only for this part of the family. Cousins and I play with LittleBrother while grownups talk. Mother and I get to talk to each other from time to time. She is getting better at speaking to me but I am not much better in return. Thick silence keeps us separated on levels that cannot be merged.

We shop before she and LittleBrother must board a plane back to Australia. She takes me to a craft store and tells me I can choose anything I want and she will buy it for me. Her offer makes me feel uncomfortable so I do not know what to say. Is she serious? Why would she be so nice to me? Too many choices in the store. She asks me what I like to do but my tongue is tied in a giant knot in the back of my throat. Bewilderment clogs my brain and I answer, "I don't know."

She removes an idea from the rack and asks if I like it. Again I am silent. She removes another idea and says Sister would like it. This does not sit well with me. She does this again and again. The more she asks me if I would like something or says that Sister would like it, the more a wall builds inside me, stopping me from blurting out, "I don't care what she likes!" It is obvious to me that she likes Sister better. Sister is more talented than me. Sister is smarter than me. Sister is more special than me because Sister got to stay with Mother. Sister was not discarded like a worn out toy or holey sock that was not worth darning.

 Mother was right. She gave away the right baby. I am broken. Mother will board her plane with LittleBrother in tow and fly off back to the children she loves. How could I attach myself to people who only bring me back into their lives to assuage their own guilt? Or was it confirmation that they made the right choice?

**

I'm no longer kept in hiding. Father and Mother opened the door that kept me concealed. Sister and Brother write and mail me letters! We eagerly await to hear from each other as blue Aerograms pass back and forth across the Pacific Ocean. We laugh and ask silly questions. We tell stories and dream of meeting each other in person one day. An empty space begins to fill inside me as I expand out and welcome my siblings into my heart. Even though we are half a globe away, I am no longer alone in this world.

Chapter 6

THE DEVIL'S SOUL

Slicing my wrist with a blade would create a gush of blood and stain the blue carpet that covers my bedroom floor. That won't do. I mustn't make messes that I can't clean up. Slipping my head through the opening of a noose and feeling the knot slowly choke off my breath will take too long. I remember the cold feel of rope around my neck as a child while living on TheFarm and refuse to put myself in that place. The memory of Grandma's neighbor hanging himself in his living room and being found by his wife flashes before my eyes. The horror that his wife and Grandma, as her friend, endured is more than I can put upon my family.

Even though I no longer wish to live, I do not want them to feel pain or cause them harm. They will be better off without me. This I am sure. I am also sure that I simply cannot continue on. Pleasing StepMom and failing to be perfect at school and home is too much. I am not that strong. Pulling the trigger on a gun aimed at my head would not work either. Dad owns rifles and the barrel is too long for me to handle by myself while pointed at my body. All of these options would hurt too. I do not wish to hurt myself. I need the pain to go away. I worry that I might mess up on killing myself and be forever stuck in greater misery.

The pain must subside soon or else I will simply die from the inside out. Running away is good in theory but there is nowhere to run. Grandma lives several miles away. The walk to her place is dangerous for a fourteen-year-old like me. Lecherous men might stop and do their best to lure me in their ratted old cars or pick-up trucks. I do not wish to be raped. I already know the horror of my virtue being threatened.

Nothing seems to be the right answer. My brain is tired of bouncing around ideas like a red rubber ball pounding against the pavement. I look out my bedroom window dormer and stare at the roof in front of me. This old converted mill is our home for now. Step-Grandad and StepGrandma let us live with them while we need a temporary space. The distance from the roof to the ground is only one story. Jumping off to my death won't work. It's not high enough. My bedroom carpet hides the path I make as I pace around my room, mulling options over and over.

At last my brain settles down and says it made a decision…I will go on living. For now. Neither Dad nor Grandma could bear the burden of my passing. I know they love me. I won't leave them. Ever. The heaviness of guilt weighs my heart so, yes, I must stay alive for their sake. I believe Dad that he did not want me to leave home and live on TheFarm when I was younger. I believe him when he tells me that I saved him as a young father and gave him a reason to live. Life was hard for him too. The least I can do is make sure he keeps living. That means I must too. But how?

I do not really wish to die. At least not fully. Only parts of me do. Parts of my head scream at me to "Get out of here!" Parts of my heart weep with confusion and acceptance that I am broken. Parts of me whisper that I need to hang on. I do not know where this voice comes from. Some moments it's thoughts that intrude and override the longing to run and hide. Other moments the thoughts come from within my chest.

**

I ride my scooter on the cement pathway that boarders our front and side yard. I stay inside the wire fence that separates the grassy area from the long gravel driveway. Left foot on the metal platform that embraces the wheels as my right foot pushes off the ground, propelling me forward. Back and forth I ride this old scooter. I know StepGrandad is upstairs in a back room. He sits there alone. Sometimes he cries. Sometimes he reads. Always, the hallway to his room sends goose bumps up and down my spine and makes the thin blond hairs on my arms stand up. Something invisible lurks in the section of space between his room and mine.

As I ride back and forth across the yard, pondering the turmoil that is my life, the answer comes to me. I know what I must do. In order to live, I will conform to and accept all the punishment that flies my way. I will stop resisting what StepMom tells me to do. I will give up and let her win. Invisible shackles latch around my legs and wrists. My spine weakens even more. My spirit to keep fighting flees. I surrender. And I agree to sell my soul to the devil that she is. It's the only way I can keep living.

**

Cramps in my gut hit me more often now. They started out of no-where but won't leave me alone. A niggling in my head says some-thing is wrong. Diarrhea hits and I rush to the toilet again. This is my secret and something I must keep to myself. We do not have money for me to be sick. I do not want to be forced to take some-thing disgusting like castor oil or any other home remedy that old wives tales swear by.

A metallic taste coats the inside of my mouth and chills quiver up and down my arms. I am tired. A lot. Now there is blood and green in the toilet. My insides knot up and I know I must tell StepMom. Even if she gets mad at me and grounds me. I must be okay. This will pass if I keep quiet. But the other side of me urges me to speak up.

I show StepMom what I found in the toilet. Her eyes telegraph that she is worried. She tells me this is not normal and she is grateful that I told her. A new softness caresses her words and sends joy to my heart. She tells Dad something is wrong and I need a doctor. StepMom does love me when I am sick. She is tender and kind and loving, but mostly only then. I love this part of her. I wish she could be this gentle with me more often. If she was, then I would return her love even more. I do love her. Oh, how I love her even though she is a monster to me. My heart begs hers to see me as her own child that she is proud of and wishes only good things for. Right now she is that mother. My fantasy mother. If only I could bottle this up and store it for when bad times hit us again like they always do.

**

Doctor sees me rather quickly. He senses urgency in not making me wait. I must pull down my pants and lie on a special table that bends so that my exposed bottom is up in the air. He carefully inserts special scissors and snips tiny pieces of my raw colon. A second doctor is with him, observing. I am their lab rat. Both men are kind and assure me they mean no harm and I believe them. I just need this to end. No one must know what is happening to me. The shame lingers inside me even though I can go home now.

He tells me and StepMom that I have a disease called ulcerated colitis. There is no cure for this disease. No one knows why a person gets it. This is something that I must live with for the rest of my life. He says it is rare for a child of my age, barely fifteen years old. He says I will have a greater chance than normal of developing colon cancer. He says I must stop drinking milk and eating corn for a week to see if this helps. If that doesn't slow the diarrhea and bleeding or if the orange pill he prescribes doesn't start to work in two weeks, then a different doctor must cut me open and remove my colon.

My insides clench up in knots over this news. A part of me begs to run and hide. Please dear God! No! This will not happen to me! I will not walk around the rest of my life with a rubber tube and a plastic bag secured to my side. I will not bear the humiliation of being the laughingstock at school. No man would want a girlfriend or wife with such a hideous attachment. No, dear God. Please, this is more than I can take. Spare my colon. Please. I am sorry for all my sins. I will be a better girl from now on. You say you will not give us more than we can handle. This is my cross to bear and I accept a humiliating disease as my punishment. Just p-l-e-a-s-e spare my colon.

Back to the hospital. Another test. I lie on the cold hard table. Bright lights cast a harsh glow around the room. A chalky white liquid solution is blasted into the depths of my gut. I need to squirm and cry out at the pressure on my insides. Tears threaten to flow but I cannot let myself cry. I must be strong and brave. Doctor and nurse hover around me, telling me to "hang on to the solution." They say if I let it go, then we must start over. Once is too much. Twice would do me in. My insides shout, "STOP!" as more and more solution fills me up and threatens to release without my consent.

At last, Doctor finally says to get up and go to the bathroom. White with swirls of red fills the porcelain toilet. I am instructed not to flush until a nurse sees what I left for her. The look on her face says all I need to know. This is not good. I am doomed. Time to get dressed and go home. I want to go home but I don't want to go home. I need to shrivel up and become invisible. My brain does not know how to handle what is happening so I let myself stop feeling. And I pretend that I am okay and paste on a smile.

StepMom is a loving saint to me through all this. She makes sure I see the doctor on time. She makes sure I have the medicine and take it every day. She makes sure we have money to pay the bills. I am so grateful for her and will be for the rest of my life. I feel a different bond with her that was missing before. Who knew that sickness would bring us together?

The medicine starts working. The bleeding stops. So does the diarrhea. My colon stays inside my body where she belongs. I hate that this is happening to me and don't understand how this part of me broke so badly. How will I cope for the rest of my life with doctors, medicine, the threat of cancer and the constant chanting in the back of my head that I might need a bag to poop in at any time?

I have to go to school but I don't tell anyone my shameful news. I can't run in gym class. Running makes me have to run to the toilet. Gym teacher asks me to join the cross country team because I am a good long distance runner. He does his best to change my mind. His dejected eyes penetrate mine when I decline. He cannot know my secret so I look away and simply absorb his disappointment in me. He is still not happy when I give him other truths such as I always have chores after school and not allowed to do anything fun until they are done. He walks away with unasked questions and disbelief on his face but he does not press the issue. For this, I am grateful.

Running the distance is something I am good at. I run inside myself every day. I run, seeking a safe hiding space inside the cavern of my psyche. When I cannot find one, I swallow anxiety and bury it deep within in safe hiding spaces, filling them up to the brim. Then I swallow even more and more until there is no more room. Must make more room somewhere and when I can't, I leave emotions dangling in the air around me, following me around rarely calling my attention. Life is simply too much to process. So I do nothing at all except hang out as if on the ceiling, watching, outside myself.

**

My eyes fly open and I jolt upright in bed. Flannel nightgown soaked with hot sweat. More sweat pools under both my small breasts. Reckless breathing starts transitioning from gasps to sporadic deep inhales. One…three…six… normal breathing returns. A rancid taste coats the inside of my mouth and I wipe warm saliva from my face. Another nightmare. All with a similar theme.

Dream…

A haunting and forceful energy pushes itself against my teenage body with a determination to penetrate my whole Being and dominate me. The presence weighs heavy on my slight frame pushing itself inside me. I fight with all my might but I'm no match for something so sinister and powerful. Once inside me, it shifts its force up to my throat and chokes me of air.

Intuitively I know that this is the Devil squeezing me from the insides out. I'm suffocating. My body is shutting down in a slow death. Darkness all around me. With a fighting will to live, I open my mouth to speak in hopes of telling the invisible force to go away. Leave me alone! Instead of my voice flowing from my lips, a sinister garbled tone forces its way out of my mouth. The words are mine but the voice belongs to something else. Pure Evil. With my last burst of effort, I somehow manage to call out, "God! Help me!" A short moment later, the terrifying force releases its death grip from my body and disappears.

I survive and wake up. Covered in sweat. Gasping for breath. Afraid to get out of bed. Afraid to crawl back under the covers.

The nightmares have become more frequent. Always the same theme: A force of evil battles to take over me, intent on suffocating me and takes away my ability to scream. How is it that I manage to call out to God for help right before I meet my demise? I'm starting to be afraid of going to sleep at night now. I worry that the devil really does own my soul.

**

StepMother dictates what I can wear to school. She doesn't care if I look like a misfit. She still controls how much food I eat at every meal. She scolds me for not eating breakfast so I gulp down oatmeal to appease her. The hot mush sits like a lump in my gut and rots. I prefer to save room for school cafeteria food, a can of soda and a bag of chips for lunch. They make me smile and give me a sense of making a choice on my own.

She tells me how to keep my dresser drawers perfect and surprises me with random searches to make sure I listen to her orders. When I fail to maintain her perfection, she dumps the contents of each messy drawer on my bed and commands that I refold and put everything back in an orderly manner.

She sneers as she tells me I cannot like boys. School dances are forbidden because as everyone who is smart knows that dancing leads to pregnancy. She tells me I am forbidden to listen to rock and roll music which is my favorite. She says the devil comes through the air waves and gets inside us. We must protect ourselves and our home from such evil. I refuse to believe her and listen to what I choose when she is not around being sure to reset the dial on the radio exactly where she left it.

I lack freedom to make many decisions on my own because most of them are made for me. Be a good soldier and I will not be punished is constantly drilled into my stubborn head. My spine is bending more and more and she scolds me for slouching. My voice is too high for her and sets her off like a fire cracker, especially if I get excited about something. I must still work on tempering myself down, not getting too happy.

She says that if we get too happy, then God will take away that happiness and teach us a lesson. She is right. Happiness never lasts for long. A force outside my power always swoops in and wipes the smile off my face and robs joy from my heart. I get what I deserve. She knows I drank alcohol and gave me one of her famous threatening, ugly faces. I didn't care. If she would have hit me, I would have laughed at her. For a short time I feel powerful and don't care what happens to me. This is a new sensation that I welcome but must promise her to never do it again. And so I tell a lie.

Chapter 7

PROPHECY AND DYING

At last, they are coming! Sister and Brother arrive from Australia. Aerograms back and forth across the mail system brought us closer and closer over the past couple of years. We three long to meet in person and dream of our reunion. What will we say once we see inside the other's soul? What will we do with our free hands that don't know where to go beyond the first hug? Will they like me for the real person I am? Or will I be a disappointment? Will they love me as their sister as I love them as my siblings?

Their plane is late and carpeting that covers the floor of the waiting area starts to spin. I do my best to keep myself upright and breathe. All I can do is temper the butterflies in my belly the best I can. Time stands still yet floats by at the same time. Perhaps it's me floating.

They exit the plane and we embrace. Sister wears the biggest smile. Brother is more reserved. Our bond is as if it were never broken. We simply restart where we left off. At least this time we are teenagers and can speak. Their voices tint every word with an accent. We laugh at each other's funny way of speaking. Brother is thrilled

91

and stunned that our roads are not littered with potholes. We laugh at this observation.

Time together flies. Sister and I dress up like twins. Even though we are 2 ½ years apart, we still look nearly the same age. With matching outfits, we are easily mixed up. I remind her that she is the older one and we laugh. We all laugh a lot together and share stories. We love each other and marvel that we are so connected even though raised half a world away. We promise to stay in contact and see each other often. We agree life is not fair that we were raised apart. We need each other.

For as long as I can remember, I've been reminded of a prophecy made when I was a baby. The message said that one day I would "return to my people for a season." Brother and Sister are my people. We are flesh and blood from the same sources. They came to me. Is this what was meant? Or is it something more?

Time together flies by too quickly. It's time for them to leave. Sister knows she must return to Australia but Brother decides to stay! He will live with us and go to school with me! He is a senior to my junior year. I am eager to show off my brother with big blue eyes like me and wavy dark blond hair. I'm confident that kids and teachers will see how special he is and embrace him.

Sister and I say a teary goodbye and promise to stay in touch. I wish she could stay too but she cannot. She is very responsible and knows that at least one of them must return to our parents.

Brother is a skilled hunter and fisherman. Dad likes these traits in a person. Now that Sister is gone, Dad spends more and more time with Brother. They laugh together and share stories. Dad's face lights up brighter than the sun when he sees Brother. They become close and closer. Their laugher does not include me. Dad no longer looks at me with joy or anticipation. His emotions are all saved for Brother. I am being pushed out of the picture and becoming a faded memory.

My brother, whom I longed to meet, who I dreamed of being my special friend, has taken my place. This option never crossed my mind. But how silly of me. I've always known that Dad dreams of having a son. Now he has one. He no longer needs a daughter. He is ripping my heart from my chest with his bare hands. Dad never really left me until now. Sending me to live on TheFarm doesn't count. His brief confession that he didn't want me shipped away rings true. He said that it was God's will. End of story. This news is filed in the archives of conversations past and sealed with imaginary "Confidential" tape. End of story. No arguing with God. Dad and I used to have an unspoken pact that we would always be together. Like Two Musketeers. That promise is officially violated.

I cannot take being shunned by Dad any longer. He must know how I feel or else I will explode into a million tiny pieces and cease to exist. With great courage I write him a letter, pouring my soul into every word along with fresh tears. I do not know what to expect from him after he reads my feelings. At least he will know that he has pushed me aside and I understand that he no longer needs me. He has all he needs now. With a heart filled with sorrow, I place the letter on his side of the bed and quietly stow away in my bedroom. He will be home before long and I'll be out of his way from now on.

Dad finds the letter and manages to read my poor penmanship. He calls to me and like a scared puppy I cower but go to him. His voice is soft when he sees me which puts me at ease. He is stunned and I see that my words sting through to his heart. He is sorry for making me feel unwanted and deserted. He assures me that I am still his daughter and he needs me too. Even though I'm taller than him, I am still his little girl. He promises to include me again. I cry and I know his heart is weeping too. His sadness leaks from his green eyes. We hug tight, heart to heart. He does love me. He just forgot for a little while.

**

Big news! StepMom announces that she and Dad are divorcing. At first I burst into tears over the announcement. My home is about to be rearranged and I have no idea what that will look like. She is touched that I show sadness over this change and assures me that everything will be okay. Ten years of her disappointment in me and Dad are about to end. A decade of pleasing and longing and seeking to take away the pain of my family, even though I caused it, is about to come to an end of sorts.

But wait. Dad is moving out, leaving Brother and me behind. He says there is no room for us where he is going. He says he doesn't want to take me away from Stepmom. Is he insane? My outburst of tears over the news of the divorce was a shock to the system and more of a knee-jerk reaction. My momentary sadness does not replace the vile loathing that stews inside me towards this woman who says she loves me as she hits me. There is no escaping her. Only Dad gets his freedom. The news is too much to process at once. He is abandoning me…again. Leaving me to fend for myself. To keep fighting and defending myself against an angry beast.

Brother and I do the best we can to weather the storm but it is too much for us. A psyche can only handle so much turmoil before it implodes. After much crying and begging, Dad makes arrangements for Brother and me to live with him. Ahh. At last. Hope is in sight.

**

Time ticks away and even though I'm a teenager, I still long to see Grandma. She is bed-ridden more and more. Coughing up phlegm day after day, year after year is taking a bigger and bigger toll on her. Her tiny body is starting to fail more now. Her heart is weakening and she can no longer take care of herself and others the way she always did.

She is a survivor of a hard childhood, slaving over a hot stove, feeding farm hands. She never complains about all the cooking and cleaning she did in her youth. Or as an adult for that matter. She took her responsibilities seriously and served her time with love for others. So much of her remains a mystery. I was too selfish to learn as much about her as I could. Now it's growing too late. I know her from my perspective but should have understood her more on the level before her life with me. To know what aspects underlie and make up her inner workings. What makes her tick.

Grandma loves everyone and wants us all to be happy and well fed. I am grateful for her teaching me to love others without expectation or conditions attached. That is how she loved and loves me. My flaws are invisible to her. She sees my smiles which are genuine for her. And she sees my heart as pure. She possesses the uncanny ability to see only love. I see and feel only love and gratitude for her. And worry.

Her sickness does not separate us on our special level. But it is growing harder and harder to see her slight frame shriveling up in her bed, lacking strength to whisper more than hello or goodbye. She always has just enough energy to acknowledge me and share a smile. Her cheeks are still tender and plump and her eyes sparkle just for me. I know I am light in her darkness. Just like she is for me. I am alive, inside and out, when I'm with Grandma.

This new phase in our lives ends the baking of pies, sewing clothes, darning socks or watching funny shows on t.v. together. No more back scratches as we snuggle in bed together, laughing and sharing secrets. No more fussing with my straggly hair to make it pretty in her eyes.

I am ashamed to say that some days I am in such pain seeing her withering away that I cannot bring myself to look at her. Her suffering is too much to bear. This hallway to the inevitable is too short, regardless of how many steps it takes to pass through. We are in denial that her days are numbered.

Perhaps if I pretend nothing is wrong, then this will change and a miracle will form before our eyes. She is my guardian angel on earth. She knew the horror of home and is the only person to speak out saying what happened to me is wrong. Her declaration always falls on deaf ears but at least I know that she cares and always did her best. My heart calls out saying, "I love you Grandma. Please don't leave me. I still need you. Forever and ever. When you die, a part of me will go with you."

**

Another school day. Not many left. Graduation is weeks away. Announcements are nearly all addressed and ready for the post office. Fleeing school once and for all is a one-way pass to freedom. No more homework. No more strict schedules. No more fighting with my alarm clock that disturbs my slumber.

Class starts and I dive into my task as the office assistant. This is an honor that I cherish and am proud to be a part of. Our school secretary chose me because I am honest and dependable. She knows that I follow orders well.

As minutes fly by, a sinking sensation hits my core. The feeling calls out to me, telling me something is wrong. I glance at the clock and note the time. A niggle settles in my gut that I cannot shake. Who is the message from? What is being said that I cannot decode?

School day ends. News faces me at home. The words that Grandma is in the hospital punches me in the chest and I catch my breath. Now I understand that she sent me this message. Her SOS reached me but I could do nothing except follow routine as if all was well.

Time passes and Grandma gets worse. Worry builds inside and all around me. We meet other family at St. Peter's hospital. The waiting room is tiny and barely holds all of us. Cousins, Aunts, Uncles fill the seats along with me and Dad. The doctor is solemn and says it doesn't look good. He grants us permission to enter her room and say our final farewell. This is too much to handle for any of us. Tears. Tears everywhere. No one is prepared to lose Grandma. She is a rock in our family. Who will we be without her?

Slowly, we enter her room, mindful of not disturbing her too much. Her tiny body is nothing more than a bump on a mattress big enough to hold more of her. Her heart beats and she smiles the best she can. She knows my heart is cracking and falling outside of me. My face fights to expresses the jumble of emotions that I cannot fully process at my core. I tell her I love her and return to the waiting room so everyone has a moment with her. She worries about me clear up until her final breath. She tells Dad to tell me not to worry about her. And then…she is gone.

**

The hard wooden pews of the church fill up as mourners arrive to pay their last respects to Grandma. She is well loved and the numbers show that all will miss her. My vantage point is a few rows back from the front, on the right side. Funerals are never fun but some people seem to take the news with a happier heart. I am more frozen to my seat and my heart can barely cope. Nice words are spoken about Grandma. I marvel at all the bright and perfume scented flowers that line the stage and around her coffin. Grandma would be thrilled to see all this beauty. Flowers made her sick so it pleases me that they can honor her in death.

The reality that Grandma is hiding in the brown wooden rectangle box in front of me is too much to take in. My mind cannot fully comprehend that she is gone. The hole in my life is deeper than the Grand Canyon and not readily filled by spoonfuls of condolences. Something is said that confuses me and before I process what is happening, the lid to her casket is lifted and I see the lifeless form of Grandma exposed.

NO! NO! NO! NO! This is too much and I panic. Tears burst and I sob and sob and sob. Why didn't someone tell me this would happen? Why are they making us look at her dead body? Someone says she looks good. No! She does *not* look good. Someone foolishly plastered her soft, delicate skin with makeup. Her hair is done up all tidy and unnatural. Grandma doesn't need makeup and her hair never looked like that. She is a natural beauty and doesn't need the trappings of an artificial world. This is not Grandma. This is a wax figure from someone's imagination. I cannot look at the imposter any more. This image must be removed from my memory but instead I am afraid it is seared to my brain like cattle being branded on the farm.

We are encouraged to celebrate Grandma but I cannot find anything to be happy about. Someone needs to stop this charade and make life go back to normal. I am expected to carry on as if death happens all the time. How do you breathe when a part of you has died?

We shuffle in cars to the graveyard. A hole is freshly dug in the spring ground and waiting to bury her forever. Her casket is slowly lowered, taking her farther away from me. Dirt will completely cover her soon. She will not be able to escape. Visions of bugs and worms and microscopic vultures swarm through my head. They will slowly decompose of her once soft body. Something is eating away inside me too. I can't see what it is but I feel it. Some days it's a slow nibble. Other days chunks go missing. A part of me feels as empty as the space that Grandma left behind.

I vow to never visit her gravesite to mourn for her. For she is not really in the cavern under the grass. I won't place flowers at the head of her metal plot marker showing the space belongs to the woman who was my favorite mother. She is not there. She is somewhere else just out of reach. But she is free. At last. I dream about her smelling roses without wheezing. Of eating blackberries without her having convulsions and the purple juice dripping out of the corners of her mouth. I dream of seeing her again, feeling her embrace. Hearing her laugh as we share stories like only grandmother and granddaughter can do. I dream of seeing her angelic face light up at the sight of me. Yes, I am a dreamer. Sometimes dreams do come true.

Her belongings are divided up between family members. I am given her pink and white robe that she let me wear every time I slept over with her. It's a bit small for me to wear now that I'm grown up but her energy lingers in the fabric and I'm afraid to wash it. Don't want to risk flushing any remnants of her down the drain. I will keep this forever as a constant reminder of the woman who once filled its now empty space.

**

Pink Floyd sings, "Comfortably Numb". This is how I like to be. This is safe and love doesn't hurt so much. The bricks and mortar of my life are too heavy to carry around all the time so I bury myself in the bliss of alcohol. I tip back and swallow as the sting coats my tongue and throat. I do this often until my body can no longer hold itself up. Another breath and I tip over and melt into the floor. I close my eyes and succumb to being numb.

Drinking is a sin. I am a sinner. I am only a teenager but no longer care about the tally marks that are my scorn. I drink alcohol, listen to rock music, lost my virginity outside marriage and swear cuss words that would otherwise get my mouth washed out with soap… All sins according to the religious doctrine of my upbringing. I am going to hell and I don't care. Can hell after death really be any worse than the one I've lived inside myself? Doubtful.

Chapter 8

FLYING DOWN UNDER THE RADAR

Brother heeds the call of the Kookabura and returns to Australia. Our time together fills in many empty spaces left over from our childhood. He and I bond like only siblings can do. We tease each other. We laugh. We play. He taught me how to aim and fire a rifle. I am forever grateful for our short years together. I understand his need to return where he belongs. We all must be where we belong. Washington is my home but I am open to flying the coop one day. A deep wanderlust stirs in a drawer inside my unformed imagination that I have not fully acknowledged yet. Perhaps one day I will.

As if to maintain an unspoken equilibrium, Sister returns! She fills the void of Brother's departure. We relish in our reconnection and pick up where we left off after her first visit. We work at the same place and I drive us to and fro. My light green 1977 Chevy Camaro with a V8 engine propels us down the I-5 freeway with the thrill of speed. Faster, faster, faster. Yes, that's how I like life.

We plan our future and vie over who will be the lucky mother to bear twins. We cook hearty meals and relish in our culinary skills. We sew matching winter jackets except hers is blue and mine is red. We still pass as twins when we put in a little effort. We dream of being together forever.

News arrives that Brother is getting married. Sister is flying back to Australia to attend the wedding. She wishes I could go with her. Air fare is too expensive to cover with the income of my retail job. Not to worry, she says and offers to pay my way. I dig in my heels and refuse.

She and Dad do their best to convince me to change my mind. They heartily explain that this would be a once-in-a-lifetime opportunity. Still, I insist on staying in America. Dad uses his stern fatherly tone and tells me I am going to fly to Australia and he will kick my butt if he has to in order to get me on the plane. His earnestness tells me he must be right, but still, I have no desire to go.

Flying to Australia means leaving Dad. It means meeting Father for the first time. It is my duty to protect Dad from emotional suffering as much as possible. I worry that my meeting Father will be too hard on Dad. Besides, why would I subject myself to meeting the one man I hate?

How could meeting my sperm donor do any good? Yes, that's all he is to me. Nothing more. He hated me and rejected me. Why would he be open to seeing me now? I mean nothing to the man who refused to admit I existed for most of my life. I am nothing more than a mistake in his eyes. A thorn in his side that needed plucking and thrown in the trash.

At last Dad and Sister wear me down. I agree to be brave and fly to Brother's wedding. I'm doing this for Sister, Brother and Dad. And no one else. I insist that I will only stay for six weeks. No longer. Six weeks away is too many already. My home is here and I don't belong anywhere else…just yet.

Now I worry and fret about stepping on snakes at the airport. I know in my gut that my biggest fear of nature will be waiting to strike out and sinks its needle like fangs into my leg as soon as my nervous feet hit the tarmac. Sister assures me this will not happen but I do not believe her! Everyone knows that Australia is dripping with snakes everywhere you look and walk. They are unavoidable. I repeat and tell myself that I must be brave.

My ticket is purchased. Passport and visa in hand. Sister and I devise a plan. We won't tell anyone on the other end that I'm flying with her. My unexpected appearance, as if out of thin air, will be the biggest surprise of all. We squeal with mischievous glee as we fantasize about the looks on the faces that greet us at the airport. Oh, we are devilish in our perfect scheme. Mother, Father, Brother and LittleBrother won't know what hit them. Up and away we go!

**

Flaps up, wheels down. Breaks on. We pull up to a stop on the black tarmac, deplane down the stairs and my feet touch the foreign ground of our final destination. Nothing will be the same. A niggle in my gut reminds me that there is no turning back.

A small group of people stand, eagerly searching for loved ones to deplane. I linger a ways back from Sister, staying under the radar. Sister is smothered in hugs and excited greetings. I stand, watching, grinning, and waiting for my grand appearance. Eyes look up and Mother spots me and shrieks. We embrace and she cries tears of joy that I am here. Father's energy shifts as if a plug was pulled from him, tilting him off balance. He squeezes me and says he is happy to see me. LittleBrother found out two weeks ago that I am more than Cousin Wendy in America. He is friendly but a bit lost for words like me. Brother and I are eager to reunite and he is thrilled that I am here to help celebrate his special day. I'm happy

103

to be here too. It feels right and I'm glad I listened to the wisdom of Dad and Sister.

We drive up the narrow Gillies Highway, the winding of the road keeping me on edge. We're on the wrong side of the road! No snakes yet but plenty of twists and turns, nervous conversations and laughter. In this moment, anyone looking at us from the outside would assume we were a normal family. Little would they realize that underneath, there isn't anything normal about us at all.

I discover that I am still a secret to those in the area. We introduce me as Cousin Wendy but no one believes it. Everyone insists that I must be a sister. People here are said to be more reserved and would not understand the truth. Do any of us understand the truth? What is the truth? My truth is that I was a mistake to be disposed of. To be forgotten. If it were not for Brother and Sister being forced to hear about me, I would still be an unknown. A nobody to them or those I meet here half a world away. Now, I am nearly a celebrity of sorts with all the fussing going on. Even Father yearns to spend time with me and practically bends over backwards in my presence.

He is a skilled harp maker. His shop takes up the entire garage. I marvel at his talent as he proudly shows me his craft. We talk in chit chat, avoiding any deep and meaningful words. It's odd that I am not angry at him now. The hatred and resentment that normally surfaces when I think of him is either in hiding or dissipated.

The wedding is beautiful and I cannot believe Brother is a married man. We still banter like old times which is good. Now that the festivities are over, I am asked to stay longer than six weeks. It's nearly time for me to leave and a part of me is feeling sad about this. I'm also torn. Dad might be hurt if I leave him longer. But then again, Sister will be hurt if I leave. The tugging in my heart and soul gets stronger as the day of my departure nears. At last I know that I must listen and stay. My visa is good for six months and Father agrees to pay my way back to America when it's time for me to leave. I dial Dad from the pay phone down the road and with hesitation, I tell him I'm not coming home yet. We both knew this would happen. The prophesy came true. This is the season with my family.

**

Father likes spending time with me. We float back and forth on the front porch swing, talking as if old lost buddies. He tells me stories and asks me questions. Nothing deep or too personal. The topic of "us" is never spoken. He works hard at showing his sense of humor and catering to my likes. What I like, he likes. I like him kissing my ass. This empowers me and makes me feel in control. Here is the man who beat me inside Mother and cast me away, eagerly getting to know me. Is he sorry for what he did? Does he regret giving me away like a worthless commodity? I may never know but I sure hope so.

Giant spiders the size of biscuits climb the wall by our bedroom. Sister and I share a room and every night before turning off the light, a spider makes its way through. What is practically routine now is my screams and Mother coming to my rescue. She is braver than I am. She is even fearless when a snake crosses our path. Cockroaches scamper at the flick of the light. A frog lives in the kitchen. So does a parakeet. This land is foreign and keeps me on my toes.

Sister, Brother and I spend as much time together as possible. We know how quickly times disappears before one of us must be left behind. Mother is sweet and loving. She tells me not to swear, which, apparently I do more than I realize. I tune her out and say what I please. She tells me that ladies don't swear. I'm not a lady.

So I can do whatever the hell I want to. And I do. With a smile, of course.

Living in the tropics, and beside a lake is an adventure and something I mostly like. The only part I don't like is, naturally, the sneaky beasties. This land is foreign in more than one way. Besides driving on the wrong side of the road, the accents can be hard to decipher. A fish and chip clerk smirks at me when I ask for catsup for my French fries. I'm supposed to ask for to*mato* sauce for my chips. That sounds stupid so I keep my American way. I actually like giving the snarky girl something to complain about. She needs to get out more and realize there is more than one way to ask for the same thing. The thought that this land could have been my home is too much to really process so I keep pushing that picture out of my mind.

We take trips together as a family, exploring the wonders and beauty of our surroundings. We stay in motel rooms and eat meals out. The four of us kids jump on beds together, capturing snippets of what our childhood would have been like had we grown up together. We declare that we would have gotten into a lot of trouble. One of us is always thinking of something unacceptable to do. And we relish in our behavior. We're just kids at heart, making up for lost time.

**

Five months blow by faster than I can count days on the calendar. Sister decides to fly back to America with me! We say tearful good-byes and thank you's and board our way back to another chapter of our lives. We don't know what road we'll travel but we do know we'll be together, for at least a little bit longer. An Australia accent replaced my American dialect. People on the plane and when we land home cannot believe I am an American. But I am. Through and through.

**∗∗

Sister and I live as if we'll always be together so the news that she must return to Australia sends panic through to my core. How will I live without her? She is my other half. How will I think and make decisions without her input? She is older than me and smarter than me and I need her. She is a lifeline to my happiness. I will float away without her. She is sure this is what she must do. Once again, we are torn apart by the expansive Pacific Ocean.

**∗∗

It's time for me to decide what to do with my life. I've flitted and fluttered about long enough. I must do something productive to earn more than minimum wage. I cannot live with Dad forever. We would drive each other over the brink. After some soul searching and dreaming, I decide to work for the airlines. With the airlines, I will travel the world for free. A wanderlust is released inside me that must be satisfied. Father told me that an ancestor was a pirate. I feel his blood flowing through me as if we are a part of each other. He needed freedom on the open seas. I need freedom wherever I can get it.

I can't help but wonder if my ancestor was a bad man like all pirates are made out to be. Or was he a misunderstood outcast who roamed the open waters, seeking to fill his inner calling with love and adventure without the confines of walls and rules? I will never know for sure but I do think of him often. Perhaps his spirit is pushing me forward, giving me courage that I lack on my own. And if it's true that pirates preferred rum, then that would explain my penchant for Bacardi Rum® and Coke®

**∗∗

The underlying vibration and vow of loyalty to StepMom lingers and weaves thick threads through my life. It never leaves because I am obligated to still be her daughter even though I have my birth mother in another country. Never ending extended family dramas play out on a regular basis and I cannot handle the expectations put upon me to play emotional games. I must leave this place. Listen to an inner whisper that encourages me to fly this coop.

Western Airlines hires me for a position in Salt Lake City, Utah. I don't know for sure where that is on the map but I do know that I am moving. I call StepMom with the news. My body jumps up and down in the kitchen as I exclaim my thrilling news. She is the second person I call. She is angry that she was not number one. She tells me to settle down and not be so excited. Air is deflated from inside me. She does not like it when I get excited. She says I go overboard. I'm not allowed to be too happy. Rein it in. She is a cold shower in the snow. Even though I am twenty years old, she thrives on controlling me. And I feel powerless to stop her. I am her dog on a leash. I cannot run away fast enough.

With Grandma buried. Sister gone. There is no real reason to stay in Washington. Dad is here but the constant barrage of drama and high expectations are too much for me to carry any longer. Even though I know nothing about Utah other than it's filled with Mormons, I can't wait to pack my bags with no regrets of leaving the world I know behind. Am I running? Yes. I'm running from the demons of my past. I'm running from the chaos of the family dynamics that still loop through the players day after day. I'm running to save myself. My new life is only two weeks and a plane ride away.

**

I take my first trip as an airline employee to Hawaii. The land of my birth. The island calls me and I answer. This is natural. This is where I belong. My new motto is, "I was born in the tropics so I belong in the tropics." Oh, if only I could live here again for real. I have no idea where our boat, the *Maile Flo* moored in the harbor. But that's okay. The ocean and the sand tell me that I am close but right now all that matters is that I'm back. And the seeds to my future are planted.

Chapter 9

GIFTS FROM GOD

New husband. New truck. New house ready to be filled with laughter and adventure. Life is good and stories unfold as each day is filled with a new level of love, joy and possibilities.

At last, I am a mother! Another dream has come true. My beautiful, perfect son fills my days with unimaginable joy. He is my life now. He is my new anchor to this world. I'm no longer floating out in space, looking for a spot to tether to. I no longer wish to skydive or any other risky behavior. I must stay alive to protect and raise my gift. How did I live so long without him? I will fight for him. I will die for him. And I pray that I walk this earth a long time to witness his every move.

I vow to be the best mother that Son could ever dream of having. He will have the stable home that was my fantasy. He will never be beaten or ridiculed for anything. I am grateful that he is a boy though because I fear I would turn into StepMom if my baby was a girl. Yes, I am afraid of myself in this way. Abusing a child is what I learned is normal. But it's not. It is small minded, fear based and unjustifiable. My dream is to have two sons. That way I will be sure

111

to never be a monster. Thank you, God, for Son.

**

The unexpected turn of events is almost too good to be true. Mother moves in with us! She sells her house in Australia and plans to live in our spare bedroom for a year. She will babysit Son while husband and I work. Having her in my life will be magical. I remember spending hours and hours and hours over the course of time dreaming of a moment like this. Fantasizing of how Mother and I would reconnect as if never apart. That she would finally see what a wonderful, loving daughter I really am. Of how she would nurture me, lavish me with praise, tell me she is proud of me. Simply be the perfect mother.

At first we spend countless hours catching up on my adult life. She gushes over Son and is grateful for this union. Now, though, that the newness is wearing off and Son is growing, as with other big dreams, that's not how our life together is turning out. Instead, I'm starting to feel as if I'm *her* mother too.

Mother's year with us passes and she signs up for another with no end in sight. We are mostly glad about this. Good news is that Daughter is born! As I hold her tiny, innocent body in my arms and breathe in her perfection, I know with my whole heart and soul that I will never harm her. I can't. I'm not a monster. Grandma taught me unconditional love and that is all I feel for precious Daughter. She and Son are picture perfect in my eyes. Now I have two reasons to live for sure.

Doctor warned me months earlier that I must be aware that I could start abusing Son and Daughter when they reach the age abuse started with me. I vow to never harm either of them. When I look at them, all I see is love and purity. A part of me laughs at my fears

112

that I could ever harm such innocent, priceless gifts. That simply is not who I am. I am love. Not hate. I would rather be inflicted with pain than to see it happen to my children. They will be protected from all harm under my watch. Nothing will get past my eagle eye. Son and Daughter are my life. I revolve around them like the earth revolves around the sun. They are my universe. Their innocent, wonder-filled, and trusting eyes tell me that they love me too. They trust me with their life. They give me a reason and hope for a bright future. I haven't thought about wanting to die in a long time. Now I really want to LIVE for my children.

Some friends say I'm over protective. They say I watch Son and Daughter like a hawk and have never seen a mother as protective as I am. I gasp inside at this observation. Not that I take their judgment of my parenting as an insult, but rather, in awe that they seem to be oblivious as to what can happen to their children if they aren't protected. I never felt protected. I felt thrown into the depths of the ocean and forced to swim if I wanted to survive. Or thrown to the wolves to see if I'd be eaten. Some days I think I would have had a safer life being raised by wolves. They protect their pack.

Even though StepMom lives far away in another state, she follows me everywhere. If she is not directly criticizing me for doing something wrong, I still hear her disapproval everywhere I turn. Good God, for the life of me I cannot silence her incessant voice inside my head. Her self-righteous correction of my behaviors and life choices reside in a cuckoo clock inside my weary mind and bust out with precision timing, reminding me I am a mess-up.

Even though I do my best at being a mother, a wife, a daughter, still I am not enough. At least not in her eyes, which morphed into mine long ago. Parts of me resist this and hope to believe she is wrong. But as always, she wins. And I retreat like a whipped dog. In my mind's eye, I am a dog. A dog that is beaten and beaten and beaten. But like all dogs, I will only take so much. One day, I will grow strong enough on the inside, turn tail and bite her on her sorry ass. She will bleed and wonder what the hell happened and question how I could possibly be so cruel.

**

Son and Daughter drive me nuts today. Not a moment to myself. Going to the bathroom alone is all but a forgotten luxury. Too few hours of sleep turns me sour and I feel like a walking dead woman. Not much help around the house. Husband and Mother expect me to do so much on my own. Some days juggling so many baskets are too much to carry, and today is one of those days. If my energy and happiness level worked like a vending machine, I would be out of coins, with nothing to withdraw. The promise of a short escape with girlfriends at a toy party for Christmas in the city tonight keeps my spark lit.

Busting out of here and feeling like an adult without a herd of calves constantly suckling on me, leaving me empty, then demanding more, is my salvation. Even though it's December and snow covers the ground up here, the Salt Lake City valley is warmer and free of the frigid white. The drive should be good. I scamper out the door, reverse out of the driveway without looking back, in gratitude for the release of pressure from inside the confines of walls. And I breathe. I'm free!

**

The drive home up the canyon is dark. I praise myself for listening to the whispers inside my head to turn down a glass of wine at the toy party. The snow plows were out spreading salt as I headed down the canyon to the city. They are gone now but with the light rain, the thought that it's possible I could hit ice further up flashes in my mind.

Another voice tells me to tighten my seat belt. I don't know why Ford makes the seatbelt so it loosens up like it does. I love our little silver Ranger XLT 4-wheel drive with the maroon stripe and extended cab but the traction can be slippery on the snow and ice. Thank goodness we put three large sand bags in the bed to give weight to the back tires. It's late. Nearly 10:00pm. Husband will be going to bed. Hopefully the kids were good for him. Taking care of two babies is harder for him than me. Maybe because I want it more.

Another voice tells me to take my foot off the gas pedal. I'm doing the speed limit of 65 but slow down to 55. The bridge across the exit to Lambs Canyon is under a mile away. Once I cross that, all should be well. It gets icy. Lots of accidents happen here. But I am safe. I am warm. I'll be home in about 15 minutes.

The bridge is under my tires now…Oh, what's this? I'm slipping. I'm losing traction. It's okay, I can steer out of this. I'm calm. Yes, I'm heading to the left towards the median. Traffic is flowing downhill, headlights warning me they are coming my way. So long as I don't cross the median, I'll be fine. I'm confident I'll steer out of this, yes, nearly there, slipping the other direction now. Tires should grasp blacktop soon. Oh, okay, I'm heading off the road. It's okay. I'm still calm. Breathe and focus. Keep steering out.

Bam! I'm flying. I've lost contact with the ground. I'm turning upside down to my left, in slow motion. The thought that people die from rolling their vehicles races through my mind. I don't want to die today. The car seat beside me shows I have reason to live. "God, help me!" I cry. A sudden and unexpected peace flows over me. I remain calm and for the first time in my life, I feel a comfort that might be God. Or an angel. This new sensation carries me as I continue turning out of control. This peace assures me that I'm going to be okay. Over I go, upside down. Back up again. Thunk.

Tires on the ground. I'm no longer upside down or suspended in air. I am alive. The windshield is cracked into tiny spider webs but intact. The other three windows vanished. The outside temperature is naturally freezing but I don't notice. My brain switches into survival mode. Turn on the flashers. Turn on the flashers. Get noticed. Someone must see me. My right arm slowly and haphazardly reaches for the steering column. The button to turn on the flashers is somewhere here. My hand lacks precision as I fumble around as if I'm drunk and lost control of my movements. My insides are calm.

Being in survival mode is a skill I know well. In survival mode, you stay in control even if your insides fight to panic. In survival mode, you must be smart and always thinking. And quickly…being ready to change directions at any second.

At last the flashers engage and almost instantly out of thin air, a man appears at my missing left window. The frantic tone in his voice asks me if I'm okay. "Yes." I say, assuring him as well as myself. He breathes in and does his best to stay calm, looking at me in wonder and disbelief. Passing headlights flying past us up the slippery canyon are mixed with the headlights of a parked car illuminating the scene.

He says he watched me as I rolled upside down and landed on all four tires but could do nothing but watch. He tells me he is an off-duty police officer returning home from an event at the Governor's mansion or some such thing. He is only wearing a white button up shirt. But seconds before he tells me he is a police man, I think, "Oh, no, the missionaries found me." Having the Mormon missionaries find and hound me is one of my worries. I do not believe in their religion and pride myself in the fact that so far, even after many years of living here, they avoided knocking on my door. If they checked their records, they would see that as a teen, I briefly did join their church but quickly decided it was nothing but confining, degrading, horse-shit.

The left side of my head buzzes and I realize I smacked it on the bent metal door frame while suspended upside down. My left shoulder suffers the same blow. Tiny chards of glass litter my ears and hair. My rescuer's voice pitches higher in a state of panic as he sees the salt bags scattered on the ground and an empty car seat still strapped in. I assure him I am alone.

He tells me I am lucky to be alive. That the sand bags could have busted through the now missing back window and killed me. So could the tool box that slid under my seat. We climb into his heated car and he calls Husband to come and get me. Mother is home to watch sleeping Son and Daughter so they are not dragged out of their warm beds and subjected to the hazards of this frigid December night. My body jerks uncontrollably. Both legs and feet jump as soon as I lightly touch my thighs. Policeman says I'm in shock. Shivers come in jolts. The inside of my head spins. I worry that Husband will be frantic about me and I don't want him to panic.

Our children are too young to be without a mother. Just babies in a car seat and diapers. They would never know how much I love them. How desperately I yearned for them. How I cried and felt broken when I didn't conceive Daughter right away.

The policeman is friendly and I envision his wife and kids at home, eagerly awaiting his safe arrival. I imagine his home as warm and welcoming. He is a gentle, caring man and emanates genuine concern for me. I'm grateful he is compassionate and not scolding me. We sit and wait as he radios for backup. I refuse an ambulance because we cannot afford the cost. We must save our limited money for more important things like bills, groceries and Christmas.

His intuition tells him to pull over more to the right to avoid getting broadsided by a speeding driver. Seconds later, he shrieks, telling me we narrowly escaped a blow to the left side of his car. I am grateful to only endure one accident tonight and be spared a second. Neither of us have a seatbelt on since we are simply idling, staying warm while surrounded by snow, ice and single digit temperature.

Husband arrives. I rush to assure him I am okay and not to worry. I'm eager for hugs and gratitude from him that I am alive and able to walk away from the scene. I imagine him being relieved that he will not be a widower and carry the burden of raising two small babies alone. And that everything will be back to normal soon.

Instead, the chill of his silence freezes my heart. He refuses to utter more than a couple factual words to me. No hugs. No gratitude that I survive. He is as cold as the cutting icy wind that whips around the outside of our Honda. As we drive home he tells me he doesn't "have time for this." He is not happy with me that he will have to take tomorrow off from work and tend to the mess I created. In this moment, I realize that I am of little value to him, easily replaceable and a pain in his life.

Breath catches midway through my lungs. Husband is not known for being warm and fuzzy but never in my wildest imagination did I dream of him resenting me when I needed him most. A giant piece of my heart and soul disconnects, turns numb and…quietly dies. Silence fills the car as we continue driving home and I wonder if perhaps I made a mistake in asking God to save me. Dying completely would have been easier. After all, I would not have been the first casualty on that curve of I-80 eastbound.

Weeks drag by and still husband refuses to say he is glad I am okay. Relieved that I am alive. Instead, he sends me angry energy and acts as if the lingering fuzziness in my head and aching shoulder are not important to him. He barely speaks to me and refuses to tell his family what happened. He is embarrassed and annoyed when neighbors find out and show compassion and concern as they ask if I'm okay.

At last, I cannot take his anger at me anymore. As he showers, I quiver as I tell him through the shower curtain that when he gets done, I need him to come hug me. Tell me he is glad I am going to be okay. And that he loves me. That's all I ask.

Long minutes tick by before he finishes showering, dressing and finally finds the willpower to sit beside me on our bed, put his arm around me, and tell me he is glad that I am still here.

His words feel forced but with a tinge of honesty. Unfortunately, I realize, as his voice filters through my heart, that his attempt at nurturing is too late. The damage is done. An invisible knife not only stabbed me and cut out my heart but also cut to the core of our marriage, too deep to ever heal. Hatred for the man I love and thought loved me is stuffed deep in a box with a lock. It's what I must do to survive. It's the only way I can deal with life now. I will myself to do my best to move forward in love. It's my only choice.

**

Mother is abandoning me again. And again, she chooses Sister over me. All I hear is "Poor Sister, this." And "Poor Sister, that." Mother is eager to move back to Australia so she can be near Sister and help her with all her woes. But what about *me*? Why isn't *my* life and *my* challenges good enough to stick around and support me through? This part of me suffers deep inside and longs to scream out in anguish as my heart takes another massive blow. But another part of me stews and boils up more rage towards her and life itself that I must keep the lid on or someone, besides me, will get burned.

119

Mother's exit is actually a relief in a big way because I am tired of feeling more like her mother than she is mine. I was thrust into the role of tending and nurturing her. Not her to me. She is a disappointment on many levels. Yes, we had fun times. But right now they don't compensate for the hole in my life. Yes, we laughed. Made friendly competitions with birthday cake decorations. I always won and took great joy in being more elaborate and detailed with frosting and themes. But this pales in comparison to the pride of being her daughter that I long to hold deep within my heart.

My dream of the perfect mother does not exist for me. I am doomed in the maternal department. Why is it so hard for mothers to love me? What have I done wrong? All I know to do is not be like the ones who call me daughter.

I find myself tangled in the covers of bed, unable to sleep for weeks. Double strength Ambien does nothing to knock me out. One hour of sleep a night is all my body will agree to. Tending to Son and Daughter is like walking through fog on another planet. Conversations are lost as soon as they pass my ears. In this moment, an uncontrollable surge of hatred escapes my darkness and I call out to Mother, wishing she could hear me across the ocean.

My wish is that she hurt as much as I do. I hate her right now. I wish her to bleed like I am bleeding. To know what it feels like to have her heart surgically removed and burned in an incinerator… as if this is normal. I won't forgive her for loving Sister more than me. Yes, I loathe and resent her right now. She doesn't deserve me. I curl up in the fetal position and yell at her even louder as I pound the bed with my fists and welcome sobs of sorrowful howlings like a wounded animal purging from the depths of my gut.

**

Disease reminds me that it still controls my life. I am its prisoner with no hope of parole. Doctor tells me that my colon is doing okay but he reminds me that I have a 50-50 chance of colon cancer. That threat always lingers in the back of my mind like a Post-It note on a mirror. I lose control of my emotions as I sit in the chair across from his expansive desk. Tears stream uncontrollably as I reluctantly share with him some of my secrets. He tells me I need help and that I am depressed. For that moment I agree to his prescription that promises to make me happy but later refuse the drug. It makes me float outside my body more than I already do. My refusal to follow his orders makes him angry at me. He refuses to speak to me ever again.

It seems as if life keeps throwing shit at me and I can no longer duck. I always hated the game of Dodge Ball. This is my life, a constant bombardment of flying things that shatter and bruise my soul. Wear me down to the point of wanting to end the pain once and for all. To decide on an unconscious level to stay disconnected from life as much as possible. At least half of me. The other half must survive for Son and Daughter.

**

My nerves jangle like a ring full of keys. Cottage cheese fills the space under my skin and covers my legs and butt. A lump the size of my little finger protrudes out of my neck making me look as if I swallowed a French fry that got lodged in the horizontal position. Dragging myself out of bed every morning is like walking up hill, backwards, while carrying rocks. It is impossible to trudge through any day without a long nap. Being a mother, wife and working part time is getting heavier and heavier. I am crumbling faster and faster. Yet, I do my best to keep up the façade that I am happy.

Doctors tell me I am fine. That my exhaustion is normal and so is my rapid, out of control weight gain. They think nothing of the lump on my throat. I tell them that I am too young to feel this old. They tell me to go home and see them again in a year.

Son and Daughter are my true joy. Without them, I would no longer exist. Even though they have high demands, I long to be the best mother I can be. They must know I am always here for them and would do anything for their happiness. They are my anchors. They make me strive to be better. One side of the battle inside me is winning and a sense of urgency strikes me. I must somehow get help but there is shame in asking.

A little voice inside my gut tells me I need to ask for mental help. But I resist at first, knowing that only crazy people do this. But, I reason with myself, I must do something before it's too late. My endurance is about to come to a halt. My life is an out of control train, barreling towards a giant cliff. The brakes are on fire and my only hope of stopping is finding a mountainside to crash into.

Memories of TheFarm sneak out of hiding and torment me. My heart constricts as if it's in a vise grip. Air chokes in my lungs and is unable to escape. No one knows the horror of that place that is my secret. Other memories from childhood taunt me too. Blood. Hair brushes broken over my head. Flying hands across my young and tender face. Ears yanked. Hair pulled. Lashings and bruises on my thin legs. The threat of humiliation over being found out that I am a bad girl swirl through my head. The images take turns flashing before my mind's projector. And they loop. And loop. And loop.

Many other points of darkness vie for room to taunt me. Over and over. They nag me, saying, "Hey, remember me? I won't let you forget!" At last, I concede that I must reach out for help. I must be brave and take any backlash for my weakness. With trembling fingers, I dial and make an appointment with a mental health professional that I pray will change my life.

**

"Your hair is the wrong color," jabs StepMom in her self-righteous tone. "You parted it down the middle," she sneers with disgust. "You didn't offer me a cup of coffee," she whines like a spoiled brat. "You didn't talk to my family enough," she scolds. I hold the receiver of the portable phone to my ear, dumbfounded that this woman still, even though I'm an adult, scolds and criticizes me like an incompetent child. As if her bitching and moaning isn't enough, she takes great pride in letting me know that she and two other family members discussed my hair and it's unanimous that it is all wrong! What the hell?! Seriously? Don't they have anything better to do than sit around critiquing and insulting me? Oh, God, I hate her.

The insatiable bitch isn't satisfied with breaking my spirit as a child. No, she believes she must continue beating me with invisible fists every chance she gets. I would do anything to slam the door and throw away the key to this wretched woman but I am still obligated to be her daughter. I am indebted to StepMom for raising me when two other mothers deserted me. She is evil and I am the guilty one for being the bad daughter. The disappointment.

She scorns me for being defensive. Of course I'm defensive. I'm always on alert for her vicious attacks. What does she expect? That I'd *thank her* for her venom? I am nearly empty inside, nothing more than a shell of a woman with the burden of true and deep happiness eluding me. I must accept that profound love and joy is for others. Not for me. I sigh and acknowledge that I have nothing much else to lose, because I'm already lost.

StepMom is thrilled that I am seeing Counselor for help. She says, "You *really* need it!" She is right. But what she doesn't understand is that I am fed up with being her whipping dog. And with what little strength I have left, I take a vow to myself. What she doesn't realize is that I'm about to bite her back on her saggy white rear end.

Counselor is my savior. She is my spine where mine is broken. She loans me strength to "divorce" StepMom. Counselor assures me that I owe this monster nothing. I shake inside as I write a letter telling her that her love is too expensive and toxic. I quit. Sever our relationship in one swipe of the sword. I tell her that if she wants to be in my life, she must be nice to me and seek help for herself first. She no longer has permission to be in my life unless she changes.

Standing up to her makes me quiver inside and I live in fear of ever seeing her again. Yet a spark inside me hopes I do so I can tell her to go to hell. And I do not forgive her. She doesn't deserve me. None of my mothers deserve me. I not only hate all three of them, I hate God too. He is no different. I admit that I hate myself most of all.

Yet…a bit of confusion slips in between my thoughts and a tiny voice whispers in my ear. The voice says that maybe I am not so bad. Son and Daughter seem to love me. How could my children love me if I'm so terrible? They are happy I am here for them. Every day is another day to prove to myself that I am not like any of my mothers. I am better than all of them.

What I need is to flee this place. Pack Children and Husband and move to Hawaii. But I am grounded and can only dream about a brighter future far away from here. Dad's words from my youth remind me that God has a blueprint for all of us. We have no choice but to walk the path He laid out before us. I remind myself that we all have our crosses to bear and I must carry mine on my own, like everyone else. Even when it means I continue to blister and bleed.

Chapter 10

ANGELS AND ENERGY

A girlfriend suggests I watch a movie called *The Secret*. And I do. Over and over. A stirring of possibilities and parted darkness gives new rise inside me. A fire ignites inside my gut and the sensation of freedom knocks on my door. I have Children watch the DVD with me. They must know that the chains and obligation of living a life by someone else's order is a bunch of lies! For the first time in my life I smell power inside me that grows and grows as I fan the flames of possibilities. As of today. I. Am. In. Charge. Of. My. Life. Period.

No more bullshit that we must follow God's plan with no deviation. No more allowing someone else dictate what makes me happy. I have the power to rule my life. This new awakening changes my vibration and I begin to dream big and not care that this is considered irresponsible by some. I embrace and feed and water my imagination. My expansion begins. I will never be the same old me.

**

125

A bacterial infection invades my body and I am bed-ridden and can barely eat. Sweating, sweating, sweating. Exhaustion. The doctor gives me antibiotics and says I will feel better in a couple weeks. Instead, the drug feels like broken shards of glass butchering my colon. Blood. More blood every time I stagger to the bathroom, bracing myself, praying I don't fall. Doctor says to try other antibiotic instead.

It's been three months now of being stuck in bed. I don't have the energy to work for my copywriting clients. One is waiting for her sales letter to post on the internet. I have no energy or mental ability to be creative. I need sleep. Food is hard to take in. My hair is falling out of my head, thinning by the day. Bed is my sanctuary and my prison. Daughter looks at me matter-of-factly with a wisp of curiosity in her tone and big brown eye and asks, "Are you going to die?" I assure her I am too young and strong to die and won't leave her.

Dad visits and helps take care of me and Children. I start to feel a tiny bit better and ask for a Frosty® and small burger from Wendy's®. Solid food feels good against my tongue. A glimmer of hope springs up, and optimism that I'll pull through starts to take over.

A client asks me to fly to Las Vegas with him to attend a workshop hosted by big name copywriters. A special lady will be there too. He says I can attend for free. We are friends and we want to help each other out. I manage to hold down enough food and stop running to the toilet in time to board the plane.

What has gotten into me to be so bold? There is no question in my mind as to whether I'm going to Las Vegas or not. I'm going! A giant magnet pulls me and the beautiful, mysterious lady in the sales letter advertising the event excites me with the hope of help. Her soul and my soul introduce ourselves, and I know that I must meet this woman. She can help me. I feel this truth through and through. And so I take a giant leap of faith, fly to Las Vegas and meet GoddessHealer who is one of the main presenters. She is a Mind/Body energy healer for business seminars. She helps participants break through fears, money blocks, stress, and overwhelm.

I am one of three women surrounded by a room of men and I am the only female sitting at the front. It is important to me to be close to GoddessHealer and hear everything she says. She is gentle, loving, caring. Her words of hope and compassion whisper to my soul. Tears threaten down in my throat but I cannot cry in a room full of testosterone. She says we often feel unworthy of success and happiness. How did she know? Can she see inside my heart? Am I that transparent? I most certainly believe that I am unworthy but I want this feeling to stop. Her love is so strong that I eventually give in and cry.

We break arrows on our throat as a sign of busting through the fear. Anxiety dwells deep inside me and bubbles to the top as I breathe in courage to sign the release form before placing the silver tipped arrow at the base of my throat. But I can't help but wonder how I will explain to anyone back home why I have an arrow pierced into the concave of my throat if I fail. Breathe, breathe, breathe. The room chants and cheers me on, being the support I lack inside.

One, two, three….In a blur I step forward and snap the thin, red wooden arrow in half. I am victorious. I take my arrow home with me and keep it as a sign of courage that I didn't realize I had.

GoddessHealer and I become fast friends. She introduces us to the magic of energy and energy healing. This odd concept intrigues me and I yearn to know more. She sends me a DVD with more information about energy healing. A stirring deep within my bones sparks visions of possibilities for me.

Several months fly by and GodessHealer teaches me more about energy and healing. I learn about tapping on invisible energy veins called meridians. A DVD is sent my way introducing me to another healing style that helps heal the inner child. A voice tells me to contact a man who says he can help me heal with this even though we live hundreds of miles apart. But I am scared. I worry about what Husband or anyone else will think about me experimenting with "weird" energy stuff. A force pushes me from inside and I tell Husband that I am taking the plunge into the unknown. My first appointment over the phone with a healer in Boston is only days away.

The lump on my thyroid still protrudes from my throat, only bigger now, more like a small carrot lodged sideways. Fat still covers my body, making me even more introverted and ashamed of myself than ever before. The fast forward button to weight gain still stuck on high speed. Nap times extend to two hours a day and leave me exhausted. This has to stop and since doctors blow me off and offer no alternative, I know I must take my health more fully into my hands. And heal myself.

I'm in shock. After only four weeks of changing my diet and releasing the valve to the pressure cooker of my deepest secrets, the lump on my throat is nearly gone. I'm down 40 pounds. There is obviously power in communicating with my inner child, giving her a voice. My psyche craves even more internal attention and releasing. I'm deeply grateful to the powerful healer from Boston. He is helping me beyond my expectations. So much more to address and release though. He says my body tests positive for a massive systemic fungal infection so I must follow a strict diet. It is impossible to keep up with the weight loss. Now I'm shopping for new pants. It's a miracle. I am hooked on healing and hungry for more.

What I notice and embrace as I crack open the buried and not so buried rage and feeling like a mistake is the possibility of one day forgiving StepMom and everyone else. I'm not totally ready for that yet though. Too much hatred spews out through my tears and cries of, "Why? Why did you do this to me? Why couldn't you love me?" And to God, I ask, "Why did you make me be born? I know I'm still your biggest mistake. I know you are punishing me because that's what I deserve." I'm shocked at the extent of hatred and rage that is stuffed inside me. I've only just skimmed the surface. More waits to be released another day.

**

Healing the pain and suffering that I beat myself up with daily is becoming more of an obsession. An inner force pushes me forward seeking out more healing modalities. I become a student of many. Absorbing teachings and in turn, practicing what I've learned on others eager to heal too. The energy healing trainings that come my way all offer a level of relief. I learn about other energy centers called chakra's and birth vivaxis where our energetic attachment remains where we were born. I learn about how our organs and endocrine system store emotions. Trainers teach about linking body parts that lost communication, thus breaking down their proper function. These are all powerful, life changing tools. Each one chips away at the hardened exterior of my inner self.

I'm starving for more release and ask unseen forces for guidance. Nearly all the money I earn from working part time is reinvested in healing myself and learning how to help others, who feel broken too. This new life calling as a healer consumes me inside and out. I am happy when being the safe place for others to land. As I heal, I use what I learn to help others.

I open my throat chakra and begin to speak out loud more. Not much. But in increments. I realize that I held the belief that no one wanted to hear what I had to say, not even the walls. That is why I kept silent, stuffing, stuffing the rage and turning it into a façade of the happy little Wendy that everyone expected. Growing up, it wasn't okay to be angry. It wasn't okay to say that I was sad or hurting. I wasn't allowed to cry from the weight of the pain being too much to bear on my slender shoulders.

But now, as I press forward, more and more of me continues to release secrets that even I am surprised to find locked inside me. As I let go, I start to have a sense of joy on a level I didn't know was possible. So much more to let go of though. But at least I'm releasing. And finally, someone gives me permission to cry because they recognize and acknowledge that I do have something to cry about.

Disease still knots up my insides and my body attacks me when stress is thrown my way. No matter how hard I try I can't stop the attacks. These internal physical attacks scare me, especially when I bleed into the toilet. The prescription medicine that I've taken since high school is making me sick and toxic. My liver is struggling to keep up with the steady influx of chemicals designed to keep diarrhea at bay. But I am hopeful that doctors are wrong and I will heal myself. If not, at least I will know I died trying.

**

GoddessHealer and I become deeper friends. She sees greatness in me that I am blind to. She encourages me to keep going down my path of healing and expansion. Her spirit supports me as I shift into not only digging out the stench of decaying emotions for purging and cleansing, but also for celebrating me as I step into the bigger arena as a healer. Not only of myself. But of others who trickle in for a taste of what I experience in this new realm of possibilities.

Something big shifts inside me and I know with every sense that being a healer for others truly is my passion and purpose. My legs wobble under me as I build confidence but with every class, every healing session of my own, strength and inner knowing comes out of hiding. I see myself building a tool kit of sorts to help people with different needs. Different pains. And I naturally shift into holding sacred, loving space for them to open their hearts and let go of their suffering. But I must focus more on myself. So the healing continues.

Anger. Rage. Spite. Self-loathing. Revenge. Abandonment. Shame. All ooze out of me like weeping, giant popped blisters from childhood. The trouble is the numbers are endless. As soon as wounds open, purge and scab over, more force their way to the surface. And more. And more. And more. I am an endless waterfall of poison.

Some days are better than others. Loneliness visits me often and reminds me of the emptiness inside me that needs filling. Sugar, cocktails and salty snacks do their best to fill the void. Chocolate cake does a satisfying job. I have little shame in whittling away at a double layer cake smothered in creamy fudge frosting. One small slice each time I pass through the kitchen. Before I know it, big chunks of sublime fill my belly.

Grandma flashes through my mind with visions of our pie baking time. I feel her love in every bite of whatever is in my mouth when I allow myself to slow down and savor the moment. I know I am filling myself up with love through food and it makes me happy for this outlet. At least for a moment. Then guilt and shame threaten to spoil the bliss and acceptance of what I am. So I shovel in a little bit more. Ah, yes, hide the bitterness of life with the sweetness of sugar.

Hawaii calls me on redial but I must hit the mute button. Moving from here is impossible. Husband hates change. I hate living in this state but he has the money which means he wins. But….as I learn to speak my voice and release some of the pressure off my past, the air stirs and possibilities begin to pivot in my favor. I begin to fan the flames that illuminate my dream.

Husband may not like change but I will wither and die without it. The Law of Attraction and the universe are my magic powers that I am gaining in understanding and more clarity. I secretly dream of what I desire and feel into the state of pretending that I am already home, where I started life oh so long ago. I'm ready to take charge of even more of life and become a mighty manifestor.

Chapter 11

FIGHTING THE HURRICANES

Daughter is depressed. She is threatening to commit suicide. Precious, beautiful daughter, whom I love more than life itself, is in more pain than I know how to handle. What did I do wrong? How have I failed her as a mother? I did everything I knew to do to be good to her. To make her happy. To give her a home I wished I grew up in. But it's not enough. She is tormented by something inside her that even she can't see.

I take her to the emergency room twice. She is released but I must keep vigilant eyes on her. Clean out her room of anything she could possibly hang herself with. That's what she threatens to do. I scour her room and find a water bottle half filled with rum, no doubt from above the refrigerator. I am annoyed that she stole my alcohol but also burdened that she needed it to sooth her suffering in the first place.

Precious Daughter is more vocal about wanting to die than I ever had the courage to express. How do I help her? I can't. I need help myself. I find a lighter that she used to burn herself. She burns and cuts to relieve the pain. I don't fully understand this because I only

133

know how to stuff the chaos deep inside my body where no one can see what I really feel. She is braver than I am to express her pain outwardly.

She is at school and threatens to kill herself again. Social worker, her counselor and I squeeze into a small room at the mental health center to discuss Daughter. I tell them that she cannot come home. It's impossible for me to keep her safe. The constant vigilant eye is not enough. I need to sleep but I worry about what she might do if I turn my head or close my eyes. We agree to find a bed for her in a psychiatric hospital. We break the news to her that she is not going home tonight. She has to get help beyond what we've done for her so far.

It's dark as we drive down the winding canyon to Salt Lake City. Rain and sleet splash against the windows of the white Explorer. Wipers barely keep up with the pace. I'm not sure where the hospital is, but have the address. Finding this new, temporary home for my baby is challenging my nerves and sense of direction.

At last I find the parking lot and we enter the building, almost as if nothing out of the usual is happening. Just another doctor's appointment. Husband meets us. He had to leave work. His presence is needed for the admittance process otherwise I'd do this on my own. Like I tend to do most of the parenting anyway. What do we say at times like this? Words cannot express the pending emptiness. The guilt. The disbelief that I am about to leave my child and trust her with people I don't know. These emotions hover just outside my body, waiting for the right time to fully penetrate and knock me off-kilter.

The long and repetitious interviews and paperwork are complete. We are led to a different waiting room behind a large door upstairs. The escort needs permission to let us in. A camera watches our every move. We walk with Daughter as far as the path will let us. Now we must turn and walk away. My feet reluctantly do their best to carry my numb body. I nearly make the distance to the door that keeps us locked inside but my legs collapse and I crumble to the floor as all remaining life is sucked out of me. Heavy wailing bursts from my mouth. I shake uncontrollably and cower closer to the floor. I'm glued to the hard, cold area beneath me. Sobs of heartache and fear wrack my weary soul. How does a mother walk away and leave her baby locked behind a steel door that is controlled by someone else sitting behind a Plexiglas panel?

I feel like the Eagles' song, "Hotel California." As the line goes, "You can check out anytime you like, but you can never leave." Will Daughter ever get to leave? Do they have a spare bed? Please! Somebody, hear my silent begging. I need a bed here too. I am my own straight jacket right now.

**

Hair falls out of my head faster than I can keep a brush clean. I mask my pale complexion with makeup in hopes of hiding the weariness of a child bent on dying. She comes home now after eleven days locked up in her psychiatric prison. She is still angry and I don't understand why. I tip toe and try not to upset her. I want her to be happy. She should be happy. I love her and take good care of her. But it's not enough.

My body sways as if being blown by wind gusts but I keep putting one foot in front of the other. Breathing. Breathing. Hoping she will come around to the happy little girl she used to be. Not the rage-filled teen who glares back at me as if I'm the enemy. She feels so unloved. But why?

My insides are a mess but I can't seem to do much to calm myself down. My spirit is hopeful that I can find a solution to this problem but none seem to be the answer. I pray for Daughter. Even though I was a mistake, she was not. She was, and is, on purpose. She was always wanted and cherished and celebrated.

Son is graduating from high school in a few months. He will move away to college. I will miss him more than I can bear to think about right now. With him gone, I will have lost both children. Daughter to her own internal torment and cutting me off and Son to a new future without me. I am happy for him. But sad for me. He is my rock. He is my constant support system. Does this make me weak? I can't take much more shit being flung my way. My one big salvation is knowing that Husband and I agree to move to Hawaii as soon as Children are grown. Hope is on the horizon but we must get through this first. All will be well then. I just know it with every cell of my body.

**

We drive Son to Washington State to start his new life. It is my job to get him set up in his apartment. I haven't slept well in about a week but I must keep pressing forward, alert and happy for Son. His future lies out before him, an expanse that he gets to fill in along the way. He is smart and savvy and brave. We embrace goodbye but the cords between us pull on me and I do the best I can to stay strong in his presence.

At home, I collapse onto his bed and wail over the loss of Son. I keep reminding myself that he did not die. He is alive. Only far from home. He is alive. I will get him back. He will be a man the next time I see him but he will still be my son. Breathe. I must breathe.

How is it that two children, reared in the same home, experience life so differently? Son kept his head low, moved quietly through his teen years and is on a straight path to his destination. Daughter's path, on the other hand is more zig-zag with sharp curves, jagged mountains and teetering on the edge of destruction.

Daughter inches her way out of the self-induced emotional closet she hides in and now sees a young man. He becomes Boyfriend. He is her reason to smile now. He brings out sparks inside her that give me hope. Yet, a big part of me begins to worry what will happen next.

**

December 10th. Word comes that brother-in-law died a tragic death. Shock fills our home and we shift into busy survival mode, planning next moves. I worry about Husband losing his brother. There is never a good time for death, especially around what is supposed to be a festive time of year. Of celebration and reunion. Not separation and destruction.

Son is home from college for Christmas vacation. Having him home gives me deep joy and strength to focus on moments of real living. We as a family relish the snow, the Christmas tree, the food and laughter around the holiday. This year will be tinted with sadness though as we mourn our great loss.

Daughter calls me from school. I don't want to answer the caller I.D. since she isn't supposed to be on the phone. Maybe something is wrong. She is down in the valley at her new school. She is happy there and no more threats of suicide.

I click the button to accept her call. She is hysterical. "What is wrong?" I plead. She sobs and finally speaks just enough that I hear her say she is pregnant and sick. She must come home. My breathing is long and slow. Her words spin around inside my head. My feet pace the brown carpet in my bedroom like a soldier practicing parade maneuvers. Phone glued to my ear. For a second, I am speechless but I gain composure before she thinks I disconnect. "I'll be right there. It's going to be okay," I say. And I mean it.

Snow and sleet challenge the drive as Son and I navigate through the canyon to the city to pick up Daughter. Before buckling in for the long drive, I tell Son not to tell his father about the baby. He doesn't need to worry about facts like this while navigating a dangerous wintery road on his way home from a full day's work. As the wipers on the Explorer flip and flop before me, an *ah-ha* moment pings my brain. "Wait!" I say, "Why am I protecting him? What about me? Why do I worry more about him and other people than I do myself?" I am the one driving in the storm to rescue our daughter. I am the one who needs protection.

"Get your dad on the phone!" I command of Son. I bark out to Husband that he's going to be a grandpa and click off the phone to focus on driving. Son helps keep me calm despite the storm brewing inside me and outside both of us.

We meet Daughter at school and escort her to the parking lot. I am remembering to breathe. My long standing conviction is that if either Son or Daughter became teen parents, I would support them through an abortion. But for some reason, this no longer becomes an option in my mind. "As far as I'm concerned," I say to Daughter before climbing behind the wheel and heading home, "you have one choice."

"What is that?" Daughter naively asks.

"You're going to have a baby."

"Good," she replies. "That's how I feel too."

I'm going to be a grandma! I breathe in the still unreal news that now a new life will fill the missing number in the family dynamic. No one can take Brother-in-law's place in the family tree, but the emptiness of a space at the table will be filled with innocent laughter and wonder of the world at large.

We drive home, me doing the best I can to process the news. Girlfriends offer to console me. We meet at one of their homes. Son tags along to keep an eye on me. I down glass after glass of red wine like water and spill my news verbatim from the phone conversations to the ride home. Birth control doesn't always work but why did it have to fail for Daughter? I tip back more glasses of wine. We laugh and slur our words like only tipsy girlfriends can. More wine flows through my veins. My face is numb and I welcome this relief. I haven't had this much to drink in a while. I'm reminded of the bliss of alcohol, my friend. Escape is important right now because reality is too much to absorb.

**

New year starts with a bang as Boyfriend causes trouble. The confusion, betrayal and emotional upheaval over accusations spin our family in a cyclone. The turmoil swallows me and refuses to spit me out. Husband tells me to "be nice." I don't want to be nice! I am pissed off at the disaster destroying my family. I'm enraged inside for the pressure of betraying myself for how I really feel. Yes, I'm a master of hiding my true feelings, masquerading like a happy clown when in fact a particular moment may be stabbing me with knives and spears. But it's different now. I can handle the misleading that my face projects because my body and psyche have more storage space for lies.

Daughter is hurting because of asshole Boyfriend. He robbed her of her innocence in more than one way. He is trouble and dragging her down to the pits of a new level of hell. I hate him. I used to love him but he betrayed my family. He betrayed Daughter. He betrayed *ME*! He doesn't deserve the growing baby girl inside Daughter. I will protect both girls. No one hurts my children and gets away with it. Someone can try and bring me down but they cannot destroy my kids. But I am mostly helpless. She loves him. But I love my daughter more. I will save her and her child. I will go to the ends of the earth to save them both. Even if it kills me.

**

Blood gushes out into the toilet. Stabbing pain shoots through my gut like an ice pick stabbing an open wound. I use every healing technique I know to stop the fear of what is happening to me but nothing works. We are supposed to fly up to Seattle and see Son today but I am too weak to get on the plane. I worry that I won't make it to the bathroom in time to contain the diarrhea of red.

I cry because I need to see Son. I cry more because I am weary. I cry even more because my body is out of control. I am digging deeper and deeper into the rage that is stored inside my gut. Facing and releasing the torment is what rips me open like a tin can of spilling tomato sauce. The rage is so deep and unexpected that I can't control it.

Hatred and resentment over Father discarding me like trash, pulling me away from Mother and abandoning my home in Hawaii as a baby is more than I can process now as the memories purge like projectile vomit. Staying alive is a constant battle that I now fear I will lose.

The bleeding has to stop. I must get to Hawaii and save myself. At least long enough to say "I did it". So many other steps have to be done first. Husband says he will take me to the doctor if I want to go. No, I do NOT want to go to the doctor. But I will. I will because I cannot continue with this blood loss. It's never been this bad before. I am genuinely scared and angry. Angry at everyone. Angry at my body. My body is failing me now when I need it the most.

Raising a baby takes endless energy and Granddaughter will be here soon. My insides feel as if I rubbed a cheese grater on them then doused rubbing alcohol over the whole lot. Then struck a match. I know what the doctor will say and do. I will have to listen.

What people don't understand is that I absorb energy of those around me. The vibration of where we live is like a constant jolt of electricity running through my veins. The group consciousness towards women in general grates on my nerves and exhausts me, making me feel as if I have to fight for my right to be me. I never felt as if I belonged here. But felt trapped with work and then the duty of giving Children a stable home. We are the wrong religion, not rich enough and vote for the opposition. This state is not my real home even after more than two decades. The energy from some of the people close to us is suffocating me with their judgement. This is all compounded by the incessant drama and chaos that is created around a teen mother that is my child.

Someone tells me that I need to force the issue of giving Granddaughter up for adoption. *Who the heck do they think they are? Who are they to tell me what is best for me and my family?* I and I alone know what is best for me and my girls. Does this person not understand that giving up Granddaughter would be like denying myself or one of my own children's existences? That giving her up would be robbing my family of a special, priceless gift that will never be replaced? Putting Granddaughter up for adoption would keep up the family cycle of giving away babies. Especially girls. Too many children have already been cast from my genetic family tree. Granddaughter will not be another disposable child.

I don't fully understand yet, but I know that Granddaughter is special. She is giving Daughter a reason to live which is gift enough but she is more than that. Only time will tell the fullest extent of her purpose. The Devil himself couldn't pry Granddaughter from our family. I'll slay the mightiest demon to keep her with me. With us. She is ours.

 At least Husband and I agree that we will move to Hawaii even though the turn of events with Daughter could have stopped us. He supports my dream. I love him for this. He has no idea the gift of life he is giving me by fanning hope of getting out of this hell hole I am burning up in. I tell him I will die if I don't move from here and I'm not exaggerating. I feel myself slipping further and further away physically. More and more like a carcass with vultures closing in. Emotionally I'm hanging on by thin hairs that sway with the breeze, threatening to snap at any time.

My body is worn out from the freezing winters. I'm tired of wearing three layers of clothing to keep goose bumps at a minimum. My body temperature is lower than normal so staying warm is nearly impossible. Shivering rarely stops. Summers are hotter now too. The sun scorches my skin after a few minutes so I stay inside as much as possible. I'm a prisoner on extreme weather days.

Something else no one understands about me is the constant tempering down of the insatiable urge to wander, to be free and explore possibilities outside the confines of the imaginary lines that draw the boarder of where we live. Wanderlust beckons the free spirit inside me, making it hard to be in one place for long without withering away. Compound all of this with the onslaught of upheaval of our lives over the past few years makes me a recipe for disaster.

**

I'm back on prednisone to stop the bleeding. This makes me cranky not only because I don't want to take it but because the drug itself makes me irritable. It's a necessary evil. I must get a colonoscopy too. Doctor said he has to make sure I don't have cancer. I meet new gastroenterologist, DrK. He is not happy with the polyps and mass that he removes. Tests show cancer has not taken hold yet. But it's knocking on the door and could be let in at any moment. Fear rises inside my core and I pray. And I refuse to accept this as my fate.

Another doctor tests me and says I have a massive systemic fungal infection. I had one before and it returned after being purged. The shock on his face as he reads me the numbers from my blood test tells me this is one test where a high score is not a good grade. A special urine test shows that I am also overloaded on six heavy metals. Possibly more but the body can only show so many at a time. Chelation IV helps relieve some of this but the cost is too much to continue. I must detox the fungus but the diet drops pounds off my body until I am nothing more than a skeleton. So I give up and re-feed the microbes that own my flesh and blood. They thrive on the sugar and alcohol that is my constant drug of choice.

**

Frantic thoughts zip back and forth through my head as I plan out the endless tasks that need doing to get our home ready for market. This summer weather is helping keep me motivated to clean out under the house, paint as much as I can on the outside and host a garage sale. I'm disgusted by how much old and useless clutter is stored from years of accumulation. Why do we do this to ourselves? Toss, toss, shred, sell, donate. Keep.

Precious Granddaughter is perfect and exhausting. How did we live so long without her? Watching her birth was an incredible gift Daughter gave me. Witnessing life emerge before my eyes nearly made me faint with shock and wonder at the miracle that played out before me. Rubbing Daughter's back through the contractions, helping her breathe through insufferable pain and holding her hand as she nearly squeezed my fingers off…all priceless. Granddaughter is an angel. I gave her the first bath, secured the tiny disposable diaper and marveled, in disbelief, that something so tiny, fragile and mysterious is now a part of our life.

My mommy instincts are in constant high gear. I forget how fragile and vulnerable infants are and remember how it's hard for me to put them down. I long to cradle her all day. But I must stay focused on getting the house ready. Focus on saving myself and family from any further peril. Neighbors spew angry words toward our family because of Daughter and Boyfriend. Their judgements weigh me down and are too much to carry. This place is definitely no longer home.

I fly to Hawaii to check out apartments. The standard of living is different from here. I don't care. I will live on the beach if I have to. But I won't have to because I am learning to believe in the power of the universe. The universe knows what I desire because I express it clearly and keep reminding the powers-that-be what I really desire. With gratitude.

My to-do list is ready with what needs to be done. I designate my jobs and what I need the universe to do for me. Me paint. Universe provide money for paint and supplies. Me find carpenter. Universe provide perfect man and money for job. The list goes on and includes prequalified buyers willing to pay full price. And be the first people to make an offer on our house.

Find perfect realtor. Check. She loves our house and gives me pointers. I am a busy, some would say frantic, home seller. Maniac comes to mind. I'm hyper focused and snap when anyone suggests I slow down. NO! I will not slow down. Something pushes me from the inside to work faster, paint this room next, and call this contractor, wash these walls. Buy these supplies. Go! Go! Go! Time is of the essence. I don't understand the urgency but I listen to the calling and pushing inside me. The clock is ticking louder and louder. There is no snooze button. I must get house ready as quickly as I can manage on my own

In five months I finish readying this house. This house that holds the echo of my children's laughter. The house that called out like a beacon in the darkness to wayward animals needing a home. To children of the cul-de-sac who were hungry or needed attention. This home that we bought together 25 years ago. So many Christmases. So many birthdays. So many parties with friends. So much love. So much confusion. So much anguish. The walls are closing in on me, telling me it's time to move on. I am grateful for this house. It was my home. It was my first stable home that Husband and I created together through good times and bad. This house protected me from tears of sorrow as two neighbors died too young. This house I will miss but right now I can't think about that. Time for that later.

**

DrK is angry with me. Colonoscopy number three doesn't happen. My colon is too inflamed for the scope to safely pass so he stops the procedure. He says we need to talk about removing this part of my body forever. What DrK doesn't understand is that I don't have time for cancer or a bowel removal. He also doesn't understand that I can't wear a bikini on the beach with a bag full of shit at my side. Hawaii will save me. I feel this truth in my bones. But I also know that I'm running out of time. Like Sister reminds me, I can live in Hawaii or I can die in Utah. Right now I'm choosing to live.

**

My bullet train action pays off. Our home sells before it's officially listed. Turns out my drive to finish as soon as possible was for a reason other than I can be considered a relentless maniac. Our buyers are pregnant and tired of looking for a nest of their own. They were about to give up when word leaked about ours. They buy house sight unseen. Any longer and we would have missed these perfect people. I am proud of myself for following instincts and holding fast to my "impossible" dream.

If life was a weather report, I am fighting hurricanes with so much force still being blown my way. I'm hanging on for dear life and riding out the wind. Ducking before being knocked out. But my body is barely hanging on. The storm has to end soon.

As we fly across the Pacific Ocean, with Daughter and infant Granddaughter in tow, I breathe deep gratitude for the unfolding of a new adventure. Yes, once again I find myself only a plane ride away from a new life.

I am a mighty manifestor. Our new place has everything I told the universe was important to me. The greater proof that I have the power to co-create with the universe gives me great hope for the manifestation of perfect health, joy and peace. Daughter is torn between being excited about this move and being angry at me. She doesn't fully understand that I had to get her out of Utah to save her nearly as much as I needed to save myself. In some ways I see this as saving my whole family. But will it cost me in the end?

Chapter 12

PICKING MORE SCABS

My flesh soaks up the warm sun and at last I begin to thaw. My body no longer shivers daily, rattling my bones. Hot sand and the aquamarine ocean beckon me to sit and ponder life. The soft wind offers to blow away my cares and helps awaken the sleeping healer inside me.

I have no friends here and do not know which way is north. All I know right now is that the spark of hope that led me here is fanning into a bigger flicker. My heart and gut tell me that so long as I hang on, I will reach my destination of peace and health. How could living here provide anything but perfection and bliss?

Now that I've been here a short while, I begin to notice that the accelerator in my body is stuck on overdrive. My internal brake is damaged and slowing down is something I must force myself to do. The cadence of the island vibrates up through my feet and silently tells me it's okay to relax. The love that permeates from strangers around me signals that I am safe. Welcome home. I breathe in the reality that I am here after such a long and painful battle. My wounds are deep. Nerves raw like a downed electrical line touching a puddle of water. I simply do not know how to relax.

Being on guard, ready for attack or change in direction at a breath's notice is all I know for sure. But what I hope to be true is that I deserve this dream that I created. My dream, not only of finding myself where I originally got lost, but also of discovering what true peace and health is all about. I desire to experience this for myself, not simply live vicariously through the hopes, dreams and experiences of others in magazines and novels.

Taking care of Granddaughter and Daughter challenges me daily. My energy is in low supply. But I came here for a reason. To heal. To save myself. To live. And this I must do every day. I ask the universe to show me what needs healing next. I'm ready to release the gags and chains and cross that I've dragged through life. Being a human has exhausted me.

**

Mother and Niece visit us from Australia! Our 600 square foot apartment bursts with estrogen. Going places together is a bit like herding cats but we make the most of each moment. Swimming in the ocean with dolphins, shopping, a luau, and endless conversations.

Having Mother here is a gift of healing for me and hopefully for her too. She tells me that the harbor is different from when we first lived here. Gone are the wooden walkways that trapped Brother after he fell off the *Maile Flo*. The slips are reconfigured. Nothing is the same. Except the memories.

Parts of me wish to fully embrace her and I do as much as I can. But a part of me still holds back a level of trust. Being a mother myself, I know I should be more understanding of the torment she endured giving her flesh and blood to others. But I'm not completely there yet. Perhaps one day I'll be less judgmental and acknowledge that I put the same pressure on her to be a perfect mother that I put on myself.

I'd never let a child be cast from my arms. I'd rather be without a husband than give up that intimate part of myself. Husband reminds me I'm not fair by putting today's standards on someone like Mother who in the 1960's had to make that decision when I was born. He is right. And I am stubborn. Some wounds may simply take longer than others to heal. So I pray for more release of the past.

✶✶

The universe hears my pleas for more healing. As is my routine now, I bravely relax and allow myself to plunge into the unknown darkness. With a seemingly endless stream of old, infected wounds that still need sterilizing, what comes up next is usually an ugly surprise. Today is no different. Within moments, I'm caught off guard but welcome the mystery that begs to be revealed. My subconscious mind releases a secret, buried so deep that exposing itself opens a monster wound that hemorrhages and leaves me spent. Cell biologists are right that every event is stored in our cell memory. Any event can be relived and released through the advancement of energy techniques that I use to help me purge and heal.

Horrific sensations and images release themselves from the depths of my hell and replay on the movie screen inside my head. In an instant, I'm reliving BirthFather beating Mother while pregnant with me. The vibration of rage as he strikes us shoots through my body and rips me open like a slaughtered animal. Shock and rage spew from deep within my core. An undeniable truth is revealed. The bastard wanted me dead! He wished to abort me! Hatred purges from the depth of my gut as I demand to know, "how DARE he loath me so much without even knowing me?" More hatred for a man I barely know erupts like an angry volcano, shooting fire and destruction into the atmosphere. Tissues cannot keep up with the wailing and gushing of tears. Why does he hate me? "I hate him. I hate him. *I hate him!!*" I cry. My voice sticks in my throat but begs to scream at the top of my lungs that I hate this man! How could I have blood flowing through my veins that is linked to his?

My body wails against the pillows and I resist punching something to release the anguish. As a mother who loves her children and would die for them, logic escapes as to how a father could wish a child dead. I spit him out with every breath. I loathe this man. If he were here before me, I'd scratch his eyes out with my claws and let him bleed to death and think nothing of refusing to help him. He deserves to die and writhe in pain. He does NOT deserve me, that's for sure.

He wanted to snuff out my life and pretend that I never existed. Well, I didn't die. You aren't strong enough to do me in. Not yet anyway. I defy you and will make you pay. Yet, a niggle inside me says Father was right. I should have died. The voice reminds me that I am God's biggest mistake. Father was simply doing what God should have done in the first place…not let me live. It's impossible to breathe right now. My voice is stuck.

As this revelation of the beating comes to awareness, I see me and Mother on the floor of our boat, curled up in a fetal position. It's as if I'm watching a movie from the ceiling now. I know I'm tucked away, somewhat safe inside her. As I watch, I weep for both of us. Her pain is my pain. My pain is hers. We are forever united in pain and feeling unwanted. We are both worthless pieces of shit. No wonder I've slowly killed myself from the inside out.

Sister and I used to joke that had I not been given up for adoption, Father would have used me as shark bait. Now I believe this to be true. My death would have easily been disguised and gone mostly unnoticed to most of the world. Losing a child at sea would have made perfect sense for a family who sailed from Hawaii to Samoa. Plenty of wide open water to toss an infant that wouldn't shut its crying mouth.

Oh yes, I hate this man now more than before. My mind continues to spin, taking in all the new awareness and in my silence… I tell God that I hate him too.

Breathe, breathe, breathe.

The night is late and I know in my soul that I need to be open to more answers and dig deeper, to let whatever else needs to be healed, come forward. For hours I sit in my bedroom, snuggled up with my blanket and pillow, leaning against the dark brown wooden headboard, I pray for more answers to my biggest mystery…. the core tone that set me up for illness, poor decisions, compounded trauma and deep seeded rage that still waits in hiding, like a bomb, ready to explode at any moment.

As I sit and process what just exposed itself from the prison of my psyche, in the flash of a Nano second, I am hit with a new train of thought. A knowing from deep within as well as from somewhere outside myself that evaporated into a new truth that God never, ever, ever, ever wanted me dead…or that I was a mistake. It's as if an explosion of mixed emotions consumes me all at once. I am NOT a mistake! Believing that God wanted me dead was a lie. A lie told to me through the words and actions of others. But not the truth from God himself. I wasted all these years locked in misunderstanding.

In this moment I know the truth that I let some people abuse me and treat me like shit because that's what I thought I was. I settled for being less than who I am because I thought I was nothing. The hatred, resentment and rage that dominate the caverns of my soul and the pits of my cells must be set free.

As a healer, I understand that not all this negativity is truly mine. I understand that I absorbed and inherited Father's rage. He passed on his sense of being a failure and a mistake to me. Mix his emotions with mine and I end up with a cauldron of rot. Life has been too hard. It's time to redirect the fire within and use it as fuel to thrive.

To be alive.

How many times have I considered trading living for the peace of death? How many times have I longed to simply surrender, curl up in a ball and dissolve? I realize that dying would be easy.

As I begin to shift and ride the waves of processing the exposure of the wounds beneath this scab, for a moment I long to simply give up from exhaustion of the emotions that rise and fall. No sooner does this thought pass through my brain when another one takes charge and reminds me that Granddaughter needs me.

Giving up is not an option. I remind myself that I promised her I would always be here for her. I would never forgive myself, not even in death, if I let her down or abandoned her. I cannot leave Son either. He and Granddaughter are the only ones still alive who have never betrayed me. I cannot be the betrayer.

And so I give myself permission to continue the process of scrubbing my cell memory of the hatred, rage and wrath towards Father. I allow my feelings to begin to evaporate into thin air and be reabsorbed by the universe. I pray to God and the Universe to reveal to me what needs healing next and brace myself for the turbulent rides ahead.

**

Even though I finally realize that I deserve to live a happy, healthy, prosperous life, I still struggle with the idea of staying alive. GoddessHealer and I talk on the phone regularly. She is one of two people I can confide everything to without her thinking I am insane. BestFriend in Utah is the other. Maybe I am nuts but they always believe in me and support me. I tell GoddessHealer something that would make others run from me. I tell her I feel there is something living inside my gut. Something dark. And evil. Something that needs to be evicted in order for me to claim my life. Something so sinister that I am cautious in speaking about it. I tell her I feel as if my gut is possessed with something of the Devil. I feel in my whole body that something/someone lives inside me.

Diarrhea continues and my moods swing from elation and feeling lighter (I can breathe deeper!) to yearning to die. Many memories of great times with family and friends flash before my eyes and remind me that not all is bad. But it is impossible to fully delete the underlying negative energy that plays non-stop like a computer hiding a virus in the background corrupting files.

My body is inflamed and the nails on my ring and index finger are detaching from the nail bed. My middle finger is on fire. The nerves up and down both legs tingle and sometimes I feel a sensation all the way down to my toes. The fear of diabetes sends panic through my veins.

Sugar seduces the emptiness inside my heart and soul and wins me over yet again. I am a slave to my insatiable sweet tooth. Eating healthfully doesn't change how I feel health-wise other than whispers of guilt that I am not strong enough to keep up the vigilance. The food game is beating me up and I cannot win. Why is this so hard?

GoddessHealer says that in 99.9% of the time a person will have near instant healing once an issue is resolved. Wow, what could be going on inside me that I haven't faced? How many years and how many thousands of dollars do I have to spend to finally feel whole and not broken?

Am I expecting too much of myself? Am I clearing out so much wretched baggage that my body is struggling to process all the changes as quickly as my mind is? Or maybe I simply need to make the clear decision to keep living. Chaos begets chaos and I am a tangled web of conflict. My body and spirit are exhausted from the endless marathon of fighting, and hiding and running from the monster. Living inside myself continues to be hell.

**

Even though I've teetered on the tightrope between living and dying, I feel as if I've turned a corner and am willing to embrace life. After all, I am finally living my dream of being in an apartment in Hawaii. Our little nest has everything I asked for: an amazing view of the ocean (we see the sunset a few months out of the year from our lanai), two bedrooms, two bathrooms, pool, BBQ, good kitchen. And we're right on the bus route. However, I still drag myself through the day and run on adrenaline. No time to rest. I have Granddaughter and Daughter to rear. Still so much drama. So little energy. Raw nerves. When will I catch a break? Moving here proves to me that I am a great manifestor so why can't I manifest healing and feeling happy for more than a little while? What about…peace?

**

It's Christmas day. Sunshine welcomes this time of celebration. I should be happy today. Son, Daughter, Granddaughter and Husband are here. Instead, I am pasted to the sheets on my bed with covers wrapped snuggly around me. Deep sadness fills me from head to toe. Presents wait patiently under our three-foot artificial tree to be unwrapped with glee. Attempts at convincing myself that it's time to celebrate backfire, and I cannot get out of bed. A voice in my head says that life has no purpose other than suffering. I am fooling myself to believe that life gets any better than what I have experienced so far.

When I dream of hope, it lasts a short time and is then replaced by doubt, despair and a river of defeat. Some talk about silver linings in the storm. Why do my silver linings rust and erode like toxic weather?

Granddaughter is only a little one, yet she exudes more joy than I've ever seen in a person. No child or adult has crossed my path who is more love than her. She radiates light wherever she goes. She wanders into my room and struggles to climb up onto the bed and join me. Even though helping raise her wears me out, she is my sunshine.

She climbs under the covers and snuggles her tiny, strong body next to me. Her warmth is a welcome addition to the empty space on the mattress. Her dark blond hair styles itself from sleep. Her eyes and face light up as she looks at me with her angelic glow. She reaches out her tiny soft hand and gently touches my cheek. Her magical touch sends a jolt of love through my body and down to my gut. The deepness of the love she transmutes to me and through me is something I've never experienced before.

She is too young to speak yet her touch speaks loudly. She telegraphs that I am loved. To hang on. Life will get better. This won't last much longer. Stay strong. Since her birth I have repeatedly stated that she is a healing baby sent by the universe. She not only gives Daughter a reason to live. She gives me one too. God bless little Granddaughter. A sense of peace begins to flow through my heart. Tears trickle out of my eyes. Once again, I renew my vow to live, if for no other reason, at least for her. She is such a Light Worker. A Miracle Child.

**

Today is Dec. 29th. I'm not sure if the word melancholy is totally descriptive of what I'm feeling or not. The definition doesn't quite encompass the full range of emotions that are surging through my

155

body and brain. It's a good starting place though, I guess. Allowing myself to actually identify emotions is something I'm working on. Stuffing them without identification is my usual M.O. but that isn't working so well for me anymore. I acknowledge that I am still numb most of the time. And I still live on the ceiling, looking down at myself and life. Will I ever live in my body? This can't be normal. Can it?

I pray for help in healing more of the old wounds that still play hide and seek in my subconscious. Within moments, my body jerks and my face is covered with slobber from yet another endless stream of undefined origin. I hear and feel a message knock on the door to my soul. As I listen with curiosity I hear voices inside and outside myself. The energy of Grandma, NewMother and AuntL send me a telegram. I marvel at how even though two of them are long dead, they still have the power to communicate with me. Their voices are inaudible to the human ear but I hear them clearly and loudly. They tell me that they support me in my healing. Collectively they tell me, "We couldn't figure out how to heal, but we know you can." This surge of cosmic support now gives me renewed strength to figure out what else needs healing. In this moment, I realize that I am truly no longer alone.

I'm slowly understanding on a deeper and deeper level that I am worthy. I am worthy of love. Of peace. Of money. And living my greatest dream, whatever that may be. I am beginning to realize that had I believed that I am worthy of something better, sooner, I would not have let people treat me poorly. Instead I would have attracted other people who saw my value because *I* saw my value. I would not have bowed down to StepMom for her meager morsels of so-called love laced with her poison. I would have noticed that I am not ugly as implied most of my life. Or fat. Or stupid. Or worthless. Or a mistake. Or that it is wrong to be female. The pressing on my heart is that I must do another big challenge…forgive myself.

✷✷

Today I ponder the options of life and death. Why is it that I cannot stop this debate between my ego and my soul? I imagine being free and happy every day living in Paradise but that is not my reality. Too many internal wounds erupt for attention and healing and I am weary. Rest is not an option. I am like a shark and must keep moving or die for sure. Should I decide to end all the havoc now, all it would take is a quick hop over the metal rail of the lanai and I would quickly plunge to my death. Splat. I'd be gone. Nothing more than unrecognizable road kill for some poor innocent soul to clean up, 23 floors below. It's tempting. The torment would stop then. I'd be free to fly which is what I yearn to do.

Lying on the loveseat on the lanai, tan cushions supporting my weary body, I gaze at a giant white cloud that clumps in the blue sky. Matching blue ocean expands out before me across the way. I play the childhood game of seeing what formation is expressing itself in the clouds. A small gasp escapes my throat. It's as plain as day. Anyone could see it. A giant Phoenix soaring above the ocean. My eyes and brain register the apparition just in time before the wind blows and reshapes the Phoenix into a giant chicken. Laughter bursts up through my body and I marvel at the synchronicity of the timing and morphing of these two birds. Laughter. I've missed laughter. You are a long lost friend. Thank you for saving me today.

✷✷

My body tingles from being acidic. Oprah promotes the importance of boosting ones immune system. Mine is shot. The more I seek to heal the carnage trapped inside my cells, the sicker I become. Why is healing so hard? Why is it that others can heal themselves instantly? Or within weeks? I've consciously worked and worked and worked my rear end off healing my past and yet my body defies me still? WHY?? I hate my body for doing this to me.

I am a master stuffer of all things. But I am opening myself up like a gutted teddy bear with all the stuffing pulled out. Yet it's not enough. Yes, I am still angry. How much rage and hatred can one person carry around inside and outside themselves? How many suitcases full of loathing am I packing around that I don't even know exist?

Am I asking too much of myself to glue back together the millions of tiny shattered pieces of glass that are me? Will I ever be the bright light that I long to be? Humpty Dumpty couldn't be put back together again but a tiny voice inside me says that I must stay confident. Never ever give up. Ever! Yes, in this moment I know that I will fit each piece of the puzzle into its respectful slot. I will not be the same brilliant masterpiece that I desire to be. Rather, I'll have plenty of scars and sharper edges and countless smudged fingerprints from putting myself back together. But that's okay. My light will shine. Some say I glow now. That tells me that I will eventually glow even brighter with wisdom and a new sense of compassion and love for others.

I recognize that nurturing people is easy for me. Loving others, making them feel comfortable and knowing they are special is one of the things I do best. But what about me? Who nurtures me? Grandma used to. But she is here only in spirit form. I do not know what it feels like to be nurtured by a mother. I tell this to GoddessHealer and she suggests something totally wild, "Call upon the Divine Mother."

She suggests I listen to a YouTube video by singer Shaina Noll titled "You Can Relax Now." She suggests I listen to this song and see myself being held in the loving arms of the Divine Mother. Being dutiful, I follow her advice.

I click Play on the video, close my eyes and sink down into the softness of my bed. In my mind's eye, I see The Divine Mother hold me in her big, loving arms. She gently rocks me while smiling down upon me. She is proud of me. This new feeling unplugs a dam of stored sorrow in my heart. Tears flow like a rushing river. My heart and soul expand. I sense the supporting presence of angels around me. My whole self is engulfed in pure, perfect, unconditional female love. And I sob more.

Even if I do die soon, at least I'll die knowing I am loved by a source greater than I am and that I made it through the hard part of life. I crossed the finish line and came out still standing. As I write these words about the possibility of dying young, fire stirs inside me. Perhaps I'm starting to get my spirit back where it belongs…on the forefront of living.

**

Life doesn't have to be hard any more. Yes, I am challenged daily with raising a baby and a teenager who doesn't know if she loves me or hates me. But I recognize that I am gradually gaining more control of life. I celebrate that I am no longer the helpless, voiceless child to be pushed around, tossed aside or punished for being less than perfect.

"Divine Mother, Father God, angels, hear my prayer. Help me heal my body quickly so I can live the life I deserve. I came to evolve and reach for enlightenment and I have achieved all I can handle at this time. Please let me stay and enjoy the benefits of my hard work. I don't understand why my body isn't physically healing quicker. Perhaps I expect too much. I've been known to set high expectations. Perhaps I simply need to rest and rely on you more as well as my inner wisdom. I don't know for sure because I'm new at this."

Ego. Great big victim ego. This is it! I must get my ego under control and quit feeling sorry for myself. When I do this, my vibration will rise and I will heal faster. I must get to the bottom of the benefit of being sick, tired and threatening myself with an early exit. Yes, I really must get over myself. Stop wearing the cloak of pain and suffering and step into my brighter self. It's time to stop punishing myself for not healing "fast enough" by my standards. I must acknowledge that it took me a lifetime to create the mess I'm in. Yes, it's egotistical of me to think that I can snap my fingers or wave a magic wand and Presto! Have a healed life. Somehow, I must start appreciating the journey. Start loving myself more. This is a process that I must take like eating an elephant…one bite at a time.

**

The universe gives me a royal smackdown today. Without mincing words in the inaudible message, I know for sure that I, and I alone am responsible for the mess that was my life. And still is. My actions, desires and worthiness level all worked together to create my reality.

It's time for me take FULL responsibility for my experiences. Past. Present. And future. As a child, I longed for a mother and I got one. But I got one who treated me the way I believed I deserved: like a piece of shit and a pain in her ass. I was the pain in Father's ass. StepMom abused me. Physical abuse is how I started this life. It's what my subconscious believed I deserved. Same with other major players along the way. I see now that I did not respect myself. Therefore, others did not respect me either. This must change or else I will keep repeating patterns. Banging my head against the wall. And keep ending up with headaches and more blisters to pop.

I'm horrified as I ponder over the years at how I treated my body. Drinking the first time at age 15. Drinking till numb by age 17.

Using alcohol to mask the feelings that cried out, but had to be swallowed. Stuffing myself with sugar and junk food to fill the constant void that only chemicals or love could fill. But real love was never found in the bottom of an empty cookie jar, bag of chips or chilled cocktail.

I am so sorry for the walking disaster that is my current reality. Bricks start to crumble around my heart and warmth towards myself moves in. Yes, I acknowledge that I am taking another step towards loving me. But still, taunting voices compete for attention. Sometimes they are silenced. Sometimes they run rampant. Right now, they are neutral.

**

"The Unquiet Dead" by Dr. Edith Fiore consumes my curiosity. She explains how we can have earthbound spirit possessions and not know it. She talks about how they can enter us when our auric field is low. The destructive energies can take control of our lives and will continue to do so until we expel them. They can cause mood swings, behavior and emotional problems. Health problems too. Her test in the book suggests I have such attachments and I want them out. NOW!

GoddessHealer offers to hypnotize me and see what happens when we can work out a time. Hypnosis is not new to me so I am super excited. It is said that especially when our life force is weak, we are susceptible to low level energies that attach to us. It is said that we can pick them up in hospitals where people die, cemeteries and pretty much anywhere low vibration resides. It is also said that drinking alcohol and taking drugs opens us up for dark energies. Drugs are never my choice. But I remind myself of the alcohol baths I gave my gut, marinating toxic emotions. Week after week. Month after month. Year after year.

This also makes me remember back to being a kid and playing in the cemetery near our house. The crematorium sat behind the fence, quietly burning bodies and turning flesh into ashes. We lived in two houses, one at a time, but next to each other. Both houses needed to be exorcised of scary spirits that StepMom and I insisted followed us around, watching our every move.

Oh, and death wishes are a great way to attract dark energies of all kinds. Lucky me.

A scene from the movie A Christmas Story flashes to the forefront on my mind. I love Ralphie and his family and laugh at the same places every time I watch it. My favorite part is always when Ralphie comes home blind due to his parents punishing him by washing his mouth out with soap. He got great pleasure out of making them remorseful by "showing" them what they'd done to him.

I understand Ralphie. We shared the same fantasy of punishing our parents for their cruelness and stupidity. Ralphie dreamed of being blind. I welcomed cancer as a child. That would be my revenge and I'd teach them a lesson. Make them get on their hands and knees and beg for forgiveness for causing my death. StepMom for making Cruella de Vil from the Disney movie 101 Dalmatians look like a saint. And Dad for keeping his head in the sand and abandoning me every day, leaving me to defend myself against a villain. For not realizing that I'd had a gut full of torment, doing nothing to protect me. And for wishing for a son instead of being more grateful for the daughter who struggled to fill the role of two children.

It's nearly a new year. My intention is for 2013 to be a year of higher vibration and that there will be no room for low energies of any sorts. Bringing this subject up for discussion within myself and with GoddessHealer stirs a darkness inside me. Something is shifting and it doesn't like being identified. I know this because my bowels lose control at 5:00am and I have to shower myself off. Yes, I'm onto something. And I ask, is this the entity's way of getting my attention? I laugh and confirm with myself that I'm onto something big. Now to sort out a time for hypnosis and exploring who and what really lurks inside the darkness of my hidden spots.

**

Today is the day that GoddessHealer hypnotizes me. My spirit is eager for purging of any negativity that might be keeping me captive. A slave to unknowingly serving a dark power out of my conscious control.

We begin…

GoddessHealer calls in angels for protection, the mighty Divine Universe for guidance and all helpers of the highest good. My body melts into the cream-colored comforter of my bed and I give myself permission to relax. The security of angel's wings embrace me as I allow myself to slip into an altered state. Almost immediately, I begin to weep. Sorrow releases itself from my womb as I relive the deeply buried grief of a miscarriage at age 25. My malnourished and weakened body, unable to accept and grow another human rejected the first trimester cells that would have been my first born. I am sorry for being a failure. For not being strong enough. And for all honesty, not ready to take on the massive roll of being a mother. I am assured by telepathic voices that my child is safe. And I am forgiven. In truth, I did nothing wrong. Ever.

What I love about using energy to heal is that time is not relevant, but rather fluid. One easily transitions from now to the past with ease. Dimensions have no boundaries. Only ego and fear can block the flow of healing energy. Quantum physics begins to describe this phenomenon but until you experience this for yourself, the concept seems ludicrous. So does the possibility that entities and negative energies that are invisible to the naked eye dwell among the living. But they do. As I am finding out first-hand.

I see my young teen-self riding my big scooter on the pathway outside the farmhouse we lived in with StepGrandma and StepGranddad. They shared their large old home with us. What started out as a mill later converted into a home. Two stories of living space are worn with time and filled with modest furnishings but warm on cold rainy winter days.

Watching myself riding my scooter, as an outside observer watching a movie quickly shifts to me, being the actress in the staring roll. Without warning, or understanding the script, I cry out. "Oh, God! Oh, God! Oh, God!" Panic replaces all sense of peace and sobs gush from my lungs. I know in every fiber of my being that something indescribable is happening. The telegraph from my subconscious warns me that some secrets need to stay that way and I'm given the choice of returning to the ignorance of conscious bliss if I decide to back out now.

Curiosity, like a cat, takes over and leads me down the path of no return. I see StepGranddad sitting in his small cluttered office space upstairs, down the hall from my bedroom.

The distance between our rooms is several yards apart. A hallway starts from my room, which is in front of the house, at the top of the stairs. It continues past a room towards the back of the house that is used for storage. StepGrandad's office is at the end of the hall. A room on the left side of the hallway between mine and Step-Grandad's is used for storage. For some reason the room never had a fourth wall on the hallway side which left its contents exposed as you walk by. The space is piled with clutter from years of accumulation. StepGranddad enters his room from an outside staircase that leads from the back of the house to the second floor. I never see him enter his room from inside the house.

Dusty books stacked in random piles, rolls of fading wallpaper deteriorating from lack of use, brown hues of dilapidated décor on the walls and floor paint the room in mystery, yet ordinariness. StepGranddad is known for his clutter and unfinished projects. The room reflects aspects of his inner workings. Light from the windows cast attention to the dust particles mingling freely in the air and coating all surfaces. Nothing is ever removed from this room. Only added. StepGranddad sits and prays. He reads, perhaps his bible but I'm not sure. I know to leave him alone when he is in solitude.

The cluttered storage space between our rooms always intrigued me, yet made the hair on my arms and neck raise to attention, as if alerting me to possible invisible danger. Most days a force pushed me away from this section of the house.

Now, lying on my bed, drifting back in time, I see StepGranddad sitting in his room, hunched over slightly in his rickety wooden chair. His profile comes into focus and I am an observer just outside his line of vision. He isn't alone. Evil surrounds him. I see this through a lens separate from my third dimensional eyes. A flash of awareness confirms within me that the darkness that surrounds StepGranddad also resides inside me. Inside the dark and dying stench of my gut.

Terror nearly consumes me and I shift to familiar overwhelm, blocking out what is too much to process at once. The evil of my teenage dreams choking off my voice, suffocating me from the inside out parallels with the fear that I am reliving.

GoddessHealer calls in what we call the Big Guns of the universe and commandes the entity to return to the light. I witness as doors of another dimension open up above me and consume the angry energy, sealing the open space behind it for good. A level of safety seeps into my soul as I begin to relax.

Showers of relief, gratitude and bewilderment flow from my eyes. A message from another part of me acknowledges my fatigue and weariness from the onslaught of pain from the past that caused me to want to give up. Give up on God. Give up on life. Give up on myself. It's as if a better offer presented itself to me as a teen and I sold my soul to the devil. We pull away from the snap shot of my youth and return to present time. A sense of relief and shock take over. What the hell was that?! Breathe!

**

Even though a part of me knows that I am safe after the entity re-lease, I find myself walking on guard, ready for attack for two days. Fear that the spirit will suddenly jump out from under the bed or behind a door and grab me keeps me on high alert. The intruder of my past haunts me even though it is gone. GoddessHealer must call for universal help again to ease my frayed nerves and assure me that I am safe from all darkness. My time in a self-induced hell is over. This begs me to ask, "Will my body finally heal?"

GoddessHealer asks the universe what I need to do to heal com-pletely. The answer is that I must learn to trust and let go. Healing is up to me. I don't know how to let go and trust. Grandma was one of the few people on earth who never let me down or betrayed me as a child. With so many people showing me that trust was a fool-ish mistake, how could I possibly let go and put faith in a higher power? I felt abandoned by God and man alike my whole life. How am I possibly expected to trust now?

Grandma's spirit comes to me and comforts me. She assures me it is okay to trust. At the gentle touch of her presence on my body and soul, I open up and weep. In this moment I agree to let go and trust. At least a little. A lifetime of pain and sorrow burst forward and flow down my cheeks like rain. Grandma continues speaking to me. Not in words that a human hears with ears, but rather to my soul and my conscious self. An energetic exchange of love and assurance that all is well.

She assures me that she is always with me and always will be. She also reveals that she was an angel on earth but died early due to the toxicity of man and the human condition. Grandma also tells me that she knows I love her and that I am to know that her illness was hers. Not mine. There was nothing I could have done to save her. Saving her was not my job. My job is to be happy. To be healthy and heal myself.

Speaking with Grandma makes me realize that I really am more than a human living on earth. I am a part of a cosmic realm and family that I don't fully understand because I cut myself off from it so long ago. This new connection of belonging to a greater source outside myself gives rise to a new level of confidence. Others can continue viewing me as odd. But I no longer care. Oh, my…Husband and family better hold on by the seat of their pants because a whirlwind of change is about to blow through.

**

I am selfish. Plain and simple. Hopefully this truth will set me freer. Life is a gift to be celebrated. To be grateful for. To be shared with those who seek its beauty. Here I am, noticing how many times over the expanse of my life that I've longed for death. Wished it as my salvation. People die every day with expansive goals and plans unfulfilled. My goal is to put one foot in front of the other without collapsing.

Brother-in-law planned to see Mother-in-law one more time. But his life was instantly snuffed out with the stop of a heartbeat. Mother-in-law talked of living to be 100 years old. Instead, her tired body called time out at 98 ½. I need to look beyond right now. But I hit walls and question if I will live to be 50 years old.

Those who have worked with me say that I am a great healer. Not only of myself, but by helping others. This is my passion. Some say I am a Light Worker. That I bring joy and hope to others in the midst of their storm. The irony of me being someone's hope is not lost on me.

Hope. That is my Jiminy Cricket. Chirp, chirp, it says. No giving up. In this moment, a surge of joy fills the cavity in my chest. In my mind's eye, I see white clouds that part with the shift of the wind. A ladder that extends higher up into thick clouds is exposed. The message is to keep aiming higher. I can't see what's ahead but that is okay. Simply trust the process. Keep climbing. Higher and higher. A rush of excitement affirms that greatness is yet to come. But I must hang on. Never. Ever. Ever give up.

**

StepMom is heavy on my spirit. She is the focus of countless healing sessions where I continue to scrub my cell memory of her poison. My heart knows that I must forgive her but chunks of me are not ready yet. Surely angels and God are growing weary of my internal battle of letting her go. I cry out for help and some of the pressure is released but always, there is more. It's as if the pits of hatred for her are a bottomless cavern. For BirthFather too. And others.

I awaken from a night's sleep with a vision of my dream replaying in my minds' eye. The vividness of it makes me question whether it really was a dream or rather a visitation of souls. Either way, I credit this experience as a gift from the angels as this is the most beautiful night time experience ever in my life.

What happened…

I hear that StepMom took a picture of a real angel and sold it to a man. I wanted a copy of the picture of the angel too but was unsure about contacting her. Divine intervention took over and before I knew it, I was entering her kitchen. I set down a single shoe but kept mine on. We spoke to each other first before actually seeing each other.   S h e entered the room but I couldn't see her face. We were both apprehensive about seeing the other after such a long time apart but we hugged. We both expressed how we feared the other would not be open to seeing the other, let alone hugging.

We stood in her kitchen and hugged tightly. She had shrunk in height and bulk and felt small and vulnerable under my embrace. Her curly/bushy/thick hair was the same dark blond with highlights only less processed by hair dye. Her multi-brown colored sweater that tied in the front felt familiar and warm. The love that flowed between us was heaven-sent. I asked her about the angel picture and expressed that I wanted a copy of the photo too and would gladly pay the same price as the man.

This dream is cut short by Granddaughter bursting her way into my bedroom and announcing the start of a blessed day. I marvel at the deep level of love I feel for StepMom and will be forever grateful for this expansion of my heart and soul. For the first time, love, peace and hope between the two of us seems genuinely possible. Even if only on a spiritual plane.

**

Like Grandma, my body is super sensitive to countless foods. My index and middle finger continue to be inflamed and my nails still partly detach around the side. My touch-starved body longs for gentle human contact but I'm not sure if my skin would handle even the lightest pressure. Good news is that my hair is no longer falling out like leaves on a tree in autumn.

Internal bleeding stops for a short time, and I start to feel human again. At the notice of this improvement, I dive into poor eating. My reasoning is celebrating my successes but a part of me feels like an internal abuser rising to strike me down. Not allowing me to be too healthy. This internal battle is a constant yo-yo of my healing journey. The celebration of food and beverage backfires and bites me on the ass. Bleeding starts again. This time it is worse than before.

Will I ever fully stop abusing myself? I long to heal but perhaps this is too much. All I know to do right now is try to forgive myself and eat more healthfully again. Give my body time to expel the toxins and process the massive emotions that nearly drown me as they rise up from the pits of my purging hell.

GoddessHealer and I talk in deep levels of topics that others would stamp us crazy. We ponder and question human life and how we connect to a higher vibration. I tell her my fear that I might be losing the healing battle. Others have the ability to heal themselves but I am not that powerful. That or else I am not supposed to. Perhaps it is my punishment.

The onslaught of constant struggle and fighting inside myself to live or die makes me realize that I never feel truly safe. Instead, I am on constant guard, ready to defend myself with each breath. Fighting is all I've known since birth. Fighting for my space on Earth. Fighting for my right to live. My right to die. My right to be loved. And wanted. My right to be free. My soul cries out saying she is tired and ready to go home. Wherever that may be.

GoddessHealer tells me that my mission is to help others. To be their beacon of light. My mission is to learn to live life peacefully in the storm. The first half of my life was chaos and mayhem. Now it's time to celebrate the completion of that journey. It's time to be happy. To live in joy. She calls in the energy of the Divine Universe to show me that there was no one left to fight. The only battle now is inside myself. I've never done anything wrong. Stay strong.

**

Jan 23, 2013

I meet up with a beautiful group of people for an evening of meditation at Ke'ehi Memorial Park. The confusing trek of finding a foreign location and not knowing anyone is creating deep anxiety. I'm about to be late and that's never okay. At last I locate the right spot. My body is exhausted from serious detoxing and only being able to eat a few tablespoons of food a day. My thin frame has noticeably sunk in more. All that is left to lose of me are my bones and skin. I'd noticed that I'd lost weight over the past couple of days. My endurance supply is practically gone.

The massive park edges up against the Pacific Ocean and the sweeping views of the mountains take my breath away. The leader of the group, YogaGuruT has me sit in front of him while he scans my back. He speaks softly in a language I don't understand. He's from India so even when he speaks English, my ears strain to understand him.

His fingers walk up my spine calling out significant events in my life that are forever marked on my soul's calendar. He identifies year after year after year of trauma that left invisible scars on my timeline.

He instructs me to breathe white light into my weary body and fill my heart with love, then send out love to everyone who has ever wronged me. Faces of Father, StepMom, and boyfriends line up on my mind's movie screen. The sight of Father releases a trap door of hatred and loathing. Hatred for him hating me. Loathing for him being a coward and shipping me away from my beloved Hawaii.

As I send forgiveness and love that comes from someplace outside myself, I begin to thank Father for doing his part in allowing me to be born in Paradise. I acknowledge that this is a sacred and blessed place to return to, to heal my psyche, my soul and my human form. The expansion of forgiveness gives me a new level of hope, peace and renewed commitment to continue my turbulent healing journey.

Before leaving for the evening, YogaGuruT identifies that something major happened to me at around age 31. He is right but we don't discuss the topic and I hold the secret inside till safely behind locked doors and alone. At home, hatred for Husband begins to gurgle and surface. Hating one's husband is not allowed so mine was stuffed down into the depths of my "promise to never tell" file. Sorrow and numbness took its place. I loathe him for not caring about me after the roll-over accident that totaled our truck. Rage spews from every cell of my body over his anger at me for inconveniencing him. Bursting rage and hatred is more than my physical form can handle and my insides begin to bleed. I wonder how much violent anger a body can store in cell memory and the pits of my bowels.

I turn to a healing friend today and he helps ease the pain. I walk away from our session feeling hopeful again with a dash of excitement knowing that I am making progress. He helps me feel safer being Me, whomever I Am. I don't know the full answer to that yet. Perhaps I will one day. But first, I must continue purging the old in order to discover the new.

**

Feb 6th

Meditation is turning out to be one of the best tools for uncovering the deeper held rage/hatred that is buried and all but forgotten in the hallows of my soul and cells. Tonight is no exception to opening up the locked chambers and spewing forth what hides inside.

Before our session swings into full speed, a voice inside me repeats itself saying, "There's no going back. There's no going back." I understand the message to mean that after tonight's releasing, I will be on a different level of understanding, awareness and expectation. It's as if I am getting ready to live a totally different life from this moment on. At least a different life on the inside.

YogaGuruT guides us in meditation and says that we still hold anger towards our parents. I let myself go and welcome secrets to come forward for acknowledgement. But as my hatred bursts to the surface, I realize it is not toward any parent…*I hate God*. Yes. I admit that I *hate* God. What reasonable God would send a child to live at TheFarm where his name is revered and feared among a bunch of hypocrites? Dad told me later, when I was a bit older and more able to understand life, that it was God's will that I be sent away. I was tricked into believing it was God who helped keep me alive for those torturous nine months. But it wasn't *God*. God be damned! I kept *myself* alive. God wasn't there. He discarded and ran away from me just like all of my so-called parents.

My soul rages at God. Crying out, demanding to know why he left me to fend for myself. Demanding to know why he did not love me. Asking, "What is wrong with me? Why am I here? *How could you forsake me? I was only a child!*"

I pray and ask for the release of this poison towards a God I do not believe in any more. I plead for cleansing from the anguish of seeking healing for my soul. I beg the torment to *stop.*

As my heart and soul release the trappings of childhood sorrow, an unexpected peace moves through my Being. A voice tells me that I was never alone. God and the angels were with me all along. They protected me from further harm. They heard my cries for comfort in the confusion that was my life. They were my saviors and returned me home.

This message feels real and I trust the warm hug and soothing of my soul as I allow this to settle in. I am a hypocrite. Hearing people blame God for their suffering and torment of the human condition drives me crazy and I chastise them for blaming someone else. Yet, here I am, blaming God for what happened to me. I am no better than the next martyr.

I appeal to God and ask forgivenes for my ignorance. For my blaming Him. At last, a higher level of peace begins to fill me from the inside out. I know that I am forgiven and assured that that I did nothing wrong.

The sun sets and the air is brisk. I sit on my mat with a pillow under my boney butt. My blue hooded sweatshirt, black puffy winter jacket and fluffy socks keep me warm. But what keeps me warmer is free flowing energy. Our group is surrounded by angel's wings as YogaGuruT calls them in one at a time: The Divine Mother, Arch Angel Michael, Arch Angel Raphael, Arch Angel Gabriel and Arch Angel Uriel and more. Their power is so strong, yet soft, and my body curls up on my sand mat, and I invite this unexpected love that is flowing through my veins. My body jerks with convulsions and I sob rivers of anguish that surrenders to a pool of salve. All communication is quietly spoken on wind and breath. We continue to converse until an internal timer chimes off. My body is spent from such deep release and transmutation of raw hatred to love. My head is dizzy and light. My internal voice asks All That Is, "How can I serve you today?"

**

The more I heal, the more I feel myself open up to who I really am. Glimpses of my true power scare me. Being helpless is what I know. Transitioning from being less of a victim to taking control of myself is a constant work in progress. I worry about others embracing the real me. The one who is opening up to beliefs about God and a mighty Universe that is a threat to those around me. I wonder who will leave me, cast me out if I decide to fully declare myself a healer and healed.

Yes, I am afraid to let go and fully trust the Universe. My belief in God shifts too. I no longer see God as a singular big scary man from my youth to be feared. Instead, I see God as a collective of energies in a vast and love-filled universe. This energy bundles together under the umbrella name of God. I see God as Life.

Yes, I am betraying the teachings of my family. But I must…otherwise I will be betraying myself. This puts me at odds with the safety and acceptance of my circle of influence and history, opening the doors for them to cast judgement on me. My beliefs threaten all that they know. However, this shift in perspective also cocoons me with those who understand me and welcome me. Without judgement.

Sister and I talk on the phone. She listens to my insecurities. She tells me that she sees me standing on the edge of a cliff with my eyes shut, too afraid to jump. But when she pulls back the lens to view the bigger picture, she sees that I am not really on a big cliff.

Instead, I am merely a step away. She explains that I am afraid of something that isn't so scary or life threatening after all. In other words, I am making something bigger and scarier than it really is. She is right. Yet I still grip the side of the cliff, afraid to fully open my eyes.

**

Once again I listen to the angelic voice of Shaina Noll. This time my imagination sings "You Can Relax Now" to my inner child. As her words speak to my heart and soul, my inner child comes to life and acknowledges that we've found sister! A part of my younger self who was frozen in time back at TheFarm is alive and awake! Celebration flows down my cheeks and I call Sister to share the news. Now that all of me acknowledge that Sister is with us, a new level of bravery shifts into place and instantly I know I can and will face any and all cliffs or steps. This is because I fully have Sister's support and I can lean on her.

**

Frustration mounts at home. My voice falls on deaf ears and agitation grows. Husband and I live parallel lives. This confusion and detachment grows deeper with anger and resentment flowing both ways. We need to free ourselves of expectations but we fail. And disappoint. I turn to my deeper faith in the Universe and ask for help. Trusting someone or something outside of my seeming control is a constant battle. Yet I wonder how life would be different if only I surrendered and truly believed and let go of my timing with healing and every other aspect of life.

Would I be as sick as I still am if I learn to fully let go and trust? How would life be different? The times that I have let go, I've witnessed the beauty of timing as events unfold like real magic. Yes,

I must work on this. For I am finally starting to understand that having control is simply an illusion. A magician's sleight of hand and the disappointment of learning that I'd been tricked.

Chapter 13

PIVOTING

A blog post asks, "Who were you before getting sick?" This question strikes a nerve and must be answered. I was a broken-hearted little girl who longed to be loved, to know she was special to someone, anyone…to feel beautiful, smart and as if I mattered. Instead, I was a disposable child…not worth listening to and out of control my whole life. God damn! Damn God! I resent being dictated by adults, food, walls, clocks and other people's ideas of who and what I should be.

I'm gaining more control of my life now but I don't always know how to handle things. And I ask myself and the universe how I can be more in control. A part of me needs to scream and throw myself on the floor like an angry two-year-old. I'm angry at the magnitude of what needs healing still. And what I've overcome.

My fighting instinct is on high alert. Fighting. That's what I do. A constant battle inside me. Fighting and running. Detaching and living in numbness. Growing up, I swam in the flaming lake of hell and got burned. Some say that we preplan our life. That there are no mistakes. That our soul needs the harsh human experience for growth. If it is true that we plan this lifetime, then I must ask, "What the hell was I thinking?!"

I turn this force inside me into passion and I see myself like a mighty Phoenix. I rise out of the ashes and emerge stronger and more powerful…unstoppable. I am Wendy. Hear me roar!

**

March 2013

Dad arrives from Washington today! We started life together here nearly 50 years ago. His visit will bring healing for both of us. My body is delicate and the least bit of stress sends my insides into attack mode. Anxiety rises and robs me of my peace. My colon is inflamed and I'm constantly running to the bathroom.

I ignore my body's warning signs and guzzle mai tais to calm my jangled nerves. Before I realize what I'm doing, I've downed six cocktails. My reliable friend, alcohol, soothed and quieted the noises inside me for the night but that didn't stop the confusion inside my heart. For two days my emotions tangle like a ball of rubber bands that bounce around inside me and I can't pull apart.

I run to the toilet once, twice, three times an hour. My colon is on fire and gets hotter with each flush of the toilet. Emotions start breaking apart and forming into words. Having Dad here brings the reality of my adoption and sordid life into full circle. His being here confirms that I am not crazy. I did not make up the saga of my existence. BirthFamily really did cast me away as a baby and then sail out of the country with Brother and Sister in tow, leaving me behind to fend for myself.

So many times I wondered about the reality of my story. Now I know for sure that my memories are real. My pain and suffering are real. Husband gives me comfort and encourages me to move past the pain. Grief consumes me. Grief over the loss of BirthFamily. Loss of not growing up in Hawaii where I belong. Loss of innocence and love.

I call GoddessHealer and she prays to Mother Mary, Arch Angel Michael and my guardian angels. Mother Mary makes her presence known and assures me that I am loved. She tells me that I am not a disappointment. And that I've done nothing wrong. She says that I am a "silly girl" for thinking those thoughts. She makes it clear that I, and I alone, am my own worst enemy. I am welcome to hand over the remaining pain any time I am ready. She also tells me that I can lean on her any time. She is always here for me. And I weep.

GoddessHealer suggests that perhaps I have a level of post-traumatic stress disorder. Records of trauma still store themselves within easy grasp…always ready to replay like a record in a juke box. Pop in a coin and push a button. Instant recall eager to blare through the speakers of my brain and throughout my body. All it takes is a sight or smell and a button is pushed and I'm instantly transported back to some place long ago.

Together, we walk through a visual in hopes of resetting my brain and electrical connections down through my fried limbic system. I do this by touching the pituitary spot on my forehead; envision connecting to my pineal gland and hypothalamus. A brilliant white light flashes throughout my brain and down my spine, illuminating my system like a flood light in a darkened room. Beauty and brilliance carries itself throughout my whole system.

Rambunctious Granddaughter bursts into the room. She brings awareness to me that it's time to focus on the Now. Focus on the child that is before me. I had my turn as the baby in Hawaii. Now it's her turn. I vow to make it the best experience a *keiki* could hope for.

Granddaughter and I emerge out of my bedroom with a new lightness, peace and love in my heart. My soul sings with knowing that if Mother Mary can love me just the way I am, then dang it, I must honor her and love myself even more. Believe in myself too. Focus on moving forward. Keep attention on living, not the past which needs to be buried in the graveyard of what no longer matters.

May 2013

Today is a double bonus. It's Mother's Day and Daughter's birthday. She, even in her state of teenage confusion and torment, is a magnificent woman in my eyes. She is my greatest challenge and mighty teacher. My heart and soul grieve for her though. She inherited my DNA laced with deep trauma, self-loathing and ancestral origins. She clearly still bares the cells of my near destruction and fights an internal battle with herself that will not call a truce. And this makes her pain my pain.

Daughter punishes herself and makes life hard. Robs herself of deep joy. I desire to make her happy but I cannot. But I can and do protect her the best I know how. Maternal bear instincts rear their fierce head and the claws come out swinging when anyone dares threaten my young. I will defend and protect her, Son, and Granddaugther to my death if ever necessary.

Dad is angry at Daughter and he is acting childish. This tears a giant rift between him and me. Love for Daughter outweighs compassion for Dad and I bear my teeth at his spiteful and vengeful ways. My body lashes out in full attack mode and reacts with silver dollar size chunks of green phlegm that cough up from my lungs.

I am bedridden for three days. The rage flowing inside my body is meant for Dad but he is not the one suffering. Shocked at the hateful exchange within my family grates on the raw flesh of my tender colon. Blood gushes into the toilet. I hate him. I hate him for not being love. I hate him for robbing me of the joy that I finally shifted into. I hate him for hurting me and my family. Slabs of foundation split and shift below my feet. My world tilts sideways and I doubt that there is a patch big enough to mend the destruction.

Healing this life is like water flowing through a colander. Progress keeps falling through the holes, never sticking around and always needing to be refilled. I beg to know how much more I must endure and how much more before all the rot stored deep within me is transmuted to fertilizer so I can grow and blossom. I swear that every time peace and joy dares to show up in my life, someone comes along and steals it like a purse snatcher.

**

May 29

Time is ticking away. Everyone is asleep except me. My body is weak and weight falls off of my already bony form. Food barely passes my lips for two days. Eating is a burden. Life is a burden. Sweat seeps out of me like a sprinkler. The infection in my lungs clings like a sticky mass of glue.

I struggle out of bed. It's 1:33 am and I cautiously shuffle to the bathroom. Blood oozes out of my colon and stains the toilet paper screaming red with every wipe. My life battery is all but depleted but I force myself to waddle to the kitchen in hopes of stirring up a refreshing glass of electrolytes. I stand on the cool tiled floor, pouring a glass of water, stirring in the pink powdered mix. My head begins to spin as if on a carnival ride. My body sways like a drunk person and my conscience tells me I am about to pass out. I pray as I plod my way back to my side of the bed.

As I drop back on the satiny sheets, I begin to pray. "I resign to the fact that I will probably die during the night. My body is exhausted. There is no end in sight. Life is simply too hard. I'm a fool to think I can heal my life. Heal my health. Love myself. Be loved the way others automatically are. It's okay, Universe, if I die tonight. I'm ready to go. However…a part of me still believes that I deserve better than this.

Dear AuntM prayed to live long enough to experience peace. So far, Universe, you are granting her prayer. If you can let her live in peace, then you can honor that for me too because a tiny part believes I deserve it."

I curl up in the fetal position, take in a couple breaths and welcome the release of death, knowing I did the best I could. Exhaustion tells me I'm a night's sleep away from getting what I asked for. Death, peace and freedom. I know Husband won't miss me for long and will easily move on. Daughter will simply have to sort out her life without me. Son will be sad but he will be strong and go on. I let go and succumb to the night.

**

I live. My eyes flash open and scan the room around me. My prayer is answered! Hope swells inside and I vow to keep diligent with healing. And I will celebrate being alive!! Gratitude and the thrill of living another day spurs me out of bed, aiming to make the most of every tomorrow.

Meditation is not my strong point but I find healing through it when I sit still long enough. Today I am reminded of my dream from age eight. The young brunette boy that I found in the field of Scotch Broom with an empty gut flashes before me, calling out for attention. The horror, hope and urgency of helping this young boy makes me understand that he is important today, just like he was in my youth. An inner voice tells me to call Sister and I do. She tells me the damaged lifeless shell of a boy in my dream is me. His missing organs that were strewn out across the field as if a bomb had exploded on his inside were mine.

Sister lovingly offers to help me find my missing parts and put me back together again. First, I find my heart. My beautiful little heart lay in my hands, shattered. She looks as if someone took a sharp object and jabbed the middle of it, splintering it like fragile glass. I hold my heart in my hands, sending it love, kissing it and gently placing it back inside where she belongs. My lungs and spleen go next.

My liver is black with hatred and self-loathing. I send my liver love and prayers for releasing the pain. I watch as my liver transforms from black and thick to red and glistening. My colon is nearly unidentifiable. The long tube darkened by the burden of over-stuffing so much pain. Suffering in blackened silence. My colon holds secrets. It holds rage. It holds my calling out for love that never materialized in a form that I understood. My colon takes the longest to respond. In fact, it is so weary that it is unable to return to health by the time I carefully replace her inside me. My colon tells me she is tired but will respond to healing over time.

Now that all of my parts are restored inside, where they belong, Sister guides me in pretending to stitch up my belly, locking all of me inside. She guides me to tenderly slide my hand over the stitches and watch them disappear without a scar in sight.

Perhaps we could give Humpty Dumpty a session in self-healing and putting himself back together again after all.

June 2013

It's my birthday week and I can barely put one foot in front of the other. The river of blood stopped. Mucus is nearly cleared up from my lungs. Belly busting coughing is nearly gone. I still question whether I will make it a few more days till my 50th birthday. I give myself the gift of a healing session today. I acknowledge that the dual state of fighting for life, yet yearning to die is all I know. I am still determined to heal despite the shambles of my life and the world around me. This is a gift worth fighting for. *I am worth fighting for.*

Helping others heal as I do so for myself restores resolve to keep going. Assisting the lost souls find their path to joy and love is my passion and mission in life. I will not fail. I will succeed. I must stop walking upstream and simply flow with the path of least resistance. Unload the weight of the world off my worn out shoulders. And really open up to deeper restoration. I must stop attacking myself and letting others attack me. Life makes me sick and this must change. Stop abusing myself. It's time for the madness to stop.

What I learn from healing is to recognize patterns. I started life being beaten in utero. Then StepMom beat me, continuing the pattern. Add a dash of organized religious bullshit that God punishes us when we're bad…don't get too happy cuz God will take away the joy…always ready for attack and if I'm not being attacked, then I better attack myself. It's what I deserve. This sick, twisted view of the world says I must be punished at all times but I denounce this rhetoric. I am not bad. I am good. I am not stupid. I am smart. I am not ugly. I am beautiful. I am not weak. I am strong. And I am really starting to understand that God/Universe really does love me. *That I am lovable.*

It's time for others to stop knocking me back on the ground as soon as I pick myself up. It's time for me to stop subconsciously inflicting physical pain on myself in order to feel some semblance of being alive…less numb. Pain makes me face what needs healing. It's time to stop shooting myself in the foot for dancing.

I also learn about ancestral trauma and how we carry their experiences forward in our DNA. All it takes is a crisis in our lifetime to flip a switch that can lead to dis-ease and destructive belief systems. Our survival instincts carry over from generation to generation too and get triggered when we experience trauma. My main instincts are to run, hide and fight. Gradually, the ghosts of my genetic line start healing. And my healing is enhanced.

**

Sister arrives for a three week visit today! We ride in a white limousine cab from the airport to home. She is exhausted from her long and boring flight from Tasmania but perks up at the reality of being so far away from her land. And us together. We laugh and marvel that we see each other in the flesh instead of the usual video chat. Our short drive here connects us as if space never separated us.

Our meeting in Hawaii is two-fold. One for pure joy of reunion. And two for healing. She needs closure from our painful past, here where we started out together. And so do I. She also needs a rest from the havoc of her life.

We know our short time together will fly by so we pack every moment with as much laughter and silliness as possible. We no longer pass as twins which is a relief to us because I never wanted to look like her. Nor she like me. We explore our old stomping grounds at Ala Wai harbor. We don't know what happened to our boat, the *Maile Flo*, and speculate that she is buried with her secrets scattered on the bottom of the ocean. We are told that the harbor looks different today than when she was our back yard. Some things change, like the revamping of a harbor. But others don't, like the thick bond between sisters.

Ala Moana Park is where we parted ways over 50 years ago. We agree to walk the land and energetically find where we said good bye. This is easier than expected. Our energetic imprints still linger, stuck in time, waiting for our return. At first, we resist the spot where our old energy beckons us, a jangle of emotions sticking in our throats. Our hearts resist what we know must be faced. But at last, we resolve and concede to the past together.

We sit on the hard ground, little ants crawling around, and we breathe. Tears choke us and we cry together. We marvel at the many parallels of our lives despite the Pacific Ocean separating us. We ponder at possibilities had I not been cast away. We resolve that what happened must have been meant to be. And we stroll out of the park, hand in hand, on our terms this time. Peace and forgiveness sweeps through us. United we stand. Forever.

At home, Sister lounges, curled up on the love seat on the lanai. Sun warms the sky and cars race by on the streets below. The thick bond between us allows an opening to share our deepest fears and pains. A dark cloud forms inside my chest and guilt clogs my throat. I must beg sister for forgiveness for an unforgivable sin.

Tears mingle in my eyes as I open my mouth and a shaky, quivering voice says, "I am sorry for being born. I am sorry for what happened to you while Mother and I were in the hospital. I am sorry that the neighbor raped your tiny 2 ½ year old body. All because of *me*. Had I not been born, then nothing bad would have happened to you. *I* am responsible for the violation done to you."

Sister looks me square in the eyes, smiles, and with a love filled heart explains to me that what happened to her was not my fault. There is nothing to forgive. She assures me it is good that I am born. She does not secretly hate me. Or blame me. It is *me* who blames me.

I did not even know that I blamed myself until a healing session brought this to my awareness. Even though I was only a newborn, I picked up on the energy of Sister's horror and took it as my own. This tells me that even then, we looked out for each other and loved each other on the deepest level from the very start. It's as if we were connected before birth. And we knew life would be brutal. So we took a vow to stay connected any way we could.

BirthFather speaks of flying here while Sister is visiting but his trip is delayed. It's just as well because I'm not ready to face him yet. We talk on the phone and take stabs at mending the past. At some point soon, I will be ready to embrace his apologies but not just yet. I need to enjoy Sister first. My senses can only process so much emotion at one given time.

**

Sister is long gone back across the expanse of blue water that separated us for so much of our life. December is warm and wet. Holiday cheer buzzes through the air and my body refuses to get out of bed. It's as if I'm stuck to the sheets. No energy to move. For two days I struggle to amble to the bathroom and fall back into bed. This is the worst exhaustion. Father is coming from Australia next month and I must be well for him. Sleep, that's what I beg for. And peace. To be left alone.

Granddaughter is my sunshine and I wish I could buy her energy. Daughter is doing better and Husband still shoots energetic darts of anger towards me. My dream is to be on an island, all alone for three months. That's all I ask for. My body demands rest. But that's asking too much so I must drag myself off the mattress and push myself even harder. I pray daily for relief of my heavy domestic duties. I dream of being well and helping others do the same. I'm encouraged to help others heal, but I must take care of myself right now. Time is not my own. I pray and tell Universe/God that I need relief soon. This feels impossible.

**

Year of the horse is rounding the corner and I can tell already that it's not a Shetland pony: It's a thoroughbred! Father is flying to Hawaii from Australia to talk to me face to face. He is willing to hop a plane and travel thousands of miles while cramped into tiny, thin cushioned seats to spend time with me. Before arriving, he graciously listens as I tell him over the phone how my being cast out of the family as a baby affected me and was the antecedent to my poor health.

We cry together through the invisible wavelengths that bounce from a satellite somewhere in space. Now, after many phone calls, buckets of tears and a heart softened by an old man seeking redemption, I am ready to face the human I've loathed forever. But first, I must feel his arms around my core. To hold me tight, like only a father can do.

It's pouring down rain, and I'm soaking wet as I enter the lobby of his Waikiki hotel. Our eyes meet and he gingerly walks over to me with a limp in his right leg. We embrace and hesitate letting go. As I scan his weathered face, I see not the beast that I conjured in my head all these years. Not the abuser that attacked me inside the womb. Instead I see him as a weary man who did the best he could. His hands are my hands. We're both big dreamers. He is tender hearted and bent by the weight of the guilt he carries. He knows I've hated him but he has hated himself more.

I understand now that times were tough for him as a skinny *haole* in a young state marred by racial tensions. I understand that he was young and scared. I understand that his heart ached as much as mine but for much longer and many more reasons than I can comprehend.

I come to understand that I am Father. Hating Father is hating myself. I forgive him but can I forgive myself?

We laugh and I listen with both ears as he tells me stories of his childhood. Of the early days when I was born. We are souls celebrating our truth that we are united in more than the physical. Always have been. Always will be. At last, the yearning in my chest is filled with the knowing that my father loves me. I can really heal now. I'm free to love myself.

Father's presence heals not only us, but Daughter too. She recognizes Father's heart and soul and they bond in unexpected ways. Hearing them laugh and play with Granddaughter brings celebration of union to home.

We dream together of him moving back to the island that he loves as much as I do. We fantasize about the fun we could have together sailing, resting in solitude and making up for lost time. I like that he is a dreamer like me. Dreams have kept me alive. I pray they do him too, for a long, long, time.

**

The Universe waves its magic wand. Daughter and Granddaughter move to the mainland. This is bittersweet. Sweet because, at last I can rest. Bitter because my heart and soul are torn by their separation from me. Granddaughter is like my baby. And all mothers know the grief of losing a part of themselves. I focus on the gratitude that life is now much easier. I marvel at what seemed impossible, of me being relieved of continuing to care for two young souls, to happening as if by magic. With such grace, ease and perfect timing.

My lesson here is to ask for what my heart and soul desires, let go of timing and trust the sources that are greater than me. I ponder, like before, whether perhaps had I trusted God/Universe while in Utah, maybe I would not have gotten so sick. Controlling the situation before moving here was my mission. Yes, I wonder…what if I'd trusted.

Girls gone. Empty spare bedroom that calls my name and lures me out of the master bedroom. I sleep on the bottom bunk and take in the space that is all mine. My body is toxic and I must detox but I misread the directions and overload my already fragile immune system. Little sores swell up on my torso, itching, burning, angry red. Shingles. My contagious body gives me a reason to stay hidden in my cave. And I ponder. And pray.

Even after all the years of peeling back the layers of my Being, a voice that grows louder and louder begs to know, "Who am I?" Yes, I'm a mother, daughter, wife, healer, sister and friend. But who is Wendy? Why am I here? The questions repeat as I sit and ponder, desperate for answers.

I wake up my computer and begin to type…

Who am I?

What will my life look like now that I'm no longer hating anyone, especially myself? What will my life smell like as I go through my day to day routine…feeling my heart burst with love and joy bringing tears that gently roll over my high cheek bones?

What will my life feel like as I accept unconditional love from a soul mate who welcomes me with open arms? Without judgment. Or expectations? Who looks at me with adoration? …Who listens as if he really hears my words as they freely flow from my moist, but once cracked and silenced lips?

What will my life sound like as I move from person to person, welcoming them into my embrace of acceptance for who they are? Loving them and helping them fill empty spaces in their hearts and lungs. Who will still be in my life? Who will leave because they can't accept the new me? Who will I push away because we grate on each other causing open wounds that only time and separation can heal?

What does success and abundance look like? Is it tender lavender and yellow spring flowers popping up through the moist soil for the first time…eagerly searching the sun for nourishment. Warmth. And assurance that they did their job well? A knowing that they are beautiful and perfect in their innocence…

Is it a majestic oak tree with thick, rough branches jutting out in all directions… inviting me to climb aboard, as high as I can go without fear of falling?

Or is it a quiet picnic lunch with my soul mate. Spread out on a block pattern quilt that was stitched by loving and skilled hands… Belly laughing at silly jokes…Rolling in the fresh, thick green grass that tickles our necks and bare feet.

What will my body feel like once it has purged itself of dis-ease and fills the space with health and self-love? Will I dance across the room and pretend I'm the prima donna in a school play?

Will my heart yearn to sing out loud…off key, but with gusto, as if I'm the most angelic singer I've ever heard?

Will I savor the gift of making love with my partner like there is no tomorrow…only today? Sweating in the energy that flows between us, melding as one. Breathing in unison. Sticking together like paper and glue. Cocooned in our little space in time, safe from the outside storm.

What will my life taste like now that I've spat out the bitterness of decades past? Self-loathing no longer poisoning and dulling my taste buds. Will it taste like the salty ocean breeze on a warm summer day? Or like melting pineapple ice cream dripping down my fingers… the sweet-tart fruit stinging my tongue followed by the pool of wetness moistening my parched mouth. Will it taste like chocolate pudding, inviting me to take another bite of its gooey sweetness as it coats my soul?

Where will I go and live out my days? The world is mighty and large. Yet, only a small portion of earth calls out to me. And even then, my heart and soul are torn. Torn between the beauty. The familiarity. The feeling of being Home. And the sense of new adventure.

What will my children and granddaughter think as they watch me, discovering who I am…morphing into someone they don't recognize? Will they be open to seeing me as I am now through their own eyes? Or will they long to view me through tinted lenses of their childhood?

Will they accept me as the expression of the expansive soul I seek to unfold in front of their lives…silently showing them that they too can follow their inner calling? And discover greatness about themselves that they might otherwise be afraid to explore?

Or will they long for familiarity and safety of the harder edged ghost of my past?

Am I brave enough to discover who I am? Or do I shrink back and let others define me… keeping me in a vice grip that is safe for them but choking me of air and expansion? Am I brave enough to listen to my soul's calling to reach out. Explore. Be open to great wonders that not even my mind's eye can create from its current vantage point?

I'm not sure who I am. But I do know that I'm a brave and peaceful warrior even through the fear. My past experience in this lifetime stands beside me like an invisible partner, assuring me that I can do anything I set my focus on. It lovingly reminds me of the times I nearly let go and caved to the pressure of the pain... but instead reached inside a vast, hidden cavern and pulled out a dose of strength that I didn't know I had.

My past reminds me that I hear the sounds of a greater source guiding me, whispering throughout my Being. Assuring me that I am love. And that I deserve all that my heart desires. Egging me on to the unknown.

I am eager to experience every second as my new life unfolds out before me, like a map in which I use 64 colors of crayons to draw in the roads and terrain...Where I choose the freeway or a meandering side road that offers scenery of six shades of green and yellow that's I'd miss if I took the fast lane... Where I connect the dots. Yes, I am brave enough to live two lives in this one life time. One of pain and suffering. One of surrendering to the universe and discovering who I really am.

Do you know who you are? If not, are you brave enough to find out?

Wendy Baldwin Feb 27, 2014

Tomorrow I'm having a channeling with my spirit guides. I've never done this before but something pushed me to give it a try. It's a bit out of my comfort zone but something says it will be worth my while. The idea of spirit guides is something that, until recently, I would have balked at. With my ever growing and changing belief system, talking to an energy that is said to be my helper is a welcome addition to my healing journey. Psychic readings are not new to me but this…this is different.

**

February 28, 2014

I'm a bit nervous for my first channeling with my spirit guides today. As soon as I hear the channel's voice, I weep. Her tone is gentle and loving. She says I have two guides who wish to speak to me. And they do. They say that I am a rainbow angel with colors of gold, silver, bronze, copper, coral, pink, rose and lavender. They say that I have been digesting the illusions of man on the third dimension. I take on other people's pain in hopes of bringing healing. In part, what this means is that I love those who are deemed harder to love by others. And I love those who would otherwise not know unconditional love. It is time for me to stop this and love myself. Allow others to love me. I am a transmitter of love for everyone but myself. Love is like a stranger that scares me. I see it and beg for it but balk at letting it in when it knocks on my door.

My guides tell me that it's time for me to shift away from the deep sense of yearning and step into who I really am. They lovingly answer burning questions around love and happiness with a life partner. I am unhappy at home on a level that I fought to keep buried but is now bursting out for immediate attention. They assure me that I deserve to be happy in all areas of life. It's time to stop denying myself love. Period. I weep. A bit of my guard lets down and I struggle to absorb the vastness of what they tell me.

Love. This is the emotion and feeling that I long for, yet struggle the most to let into my heart and soul. The heaviness of the concept of letting love inside me is too much to process. An unsettling tells me to get out outside in nature. The swimming pool invites me to plunge in and let the energy from the water help me breathe in and absorb what I just experienced. I heed the water's calling and with a small splash, let Mother Nature work her magic.

I force myself to breathe in the essence of love with each arm stroke as I paddle back and forth in the swimming pool. My lungs choke in the foreign feeling as I inhale, arm rounded above my head. Exhales are heavy as each arm slices through the cool water. I push myself to take a few more laps as I practice this new intake of love. Why have I denied myself so much?

I struggle admitting that I am not happy in marriage and haven't been for a long time. Am I selfish for yearning for deep happiness in all areas of life? Do I stick with a commitment that I made at age 25 that now grates on my psyche and keeps my nerves on high alert, always ready to defend myself? My guides said "No." I choose to believe them.

Husband and I barely speak and when we do, it's not mixed with love, but rather loathing. I am an overcooked goose. With fried nerves, I muster courage and exit our marriage. Guilt laces the words I use to express my angst. Yet a drop of hope stays visible enough to keep me solid in my conviction. Love is all I seek. Even between us, now and forever. But love comes in many forms and many levels. Romantic love is replaced by gratitude for a man who did his best and loved me the only way he knew how. I have outgrown our marriage and this truth will set us both free.

At last I am unrestricted to express buried torment from our past. He listens and holds me as I sob on his strong chest. His arms protect me like I've longed for. This makes me question, why couldn't we be like this before? Why does it take separation to bring us closer together?

Now, instead of clashing like titans or the screech of fingernails on the chalk board, we unite in respect and honor. We agree to stand united for our family. To support each other like never before. And always come from a state of support. I love Husband and he loves me enough to let me go.

With a mix of sadness and hope, our divorce is sealed. We don't talk about this life change more than necessary and slowly leak our message to friends and family. There is beauty in the sadness of divorce though. Husband and I communicate, we cheer each other on. We desire only the best for the other. People comment that we had the only peaceful, loving divorce they had ever seen. This is something we can pride ourselves in. We will forever be in each other's lives on some level…friends, parents and grandparents. And for a time, roommates.

**

Deep healing continues. The pits of my belly bubble up images of Utah. People who caused unbearable stress flash before my eyes. Loathing towards them spills from my lips and I sit on my bed to write them a letter laced with scorn and revenge. Words on paper will have to suffice. For what I deeply wish for is to lash out at them with fists. I pick up pen and position paper to begin the unloading of my wrath.

To my surprise, instead of ink spelling out cursings and rantings, I begin to write a love letter to Daughter. My higher self takes over and forgives those who, only seconds ago were lined up in my crosshairs. I write the following…

My Dearest Daughter,

I am so sorry for whatever happened in your life that caused so much anguish that you wanted to die. I'm so sorry I couldn't take away your pain and suffering and make it my own – to spare you the grief, sorrow and longing to know you are loved. And worthy.

I am so sorry I wasn't a better mother with a magic wand to wave before your eyes so you could instantly see your beauty. Your magnificence. Your brilliance. I'm so sorry you have to go down the pain-filled path of self-discovery like I did. I dreamed and hoped and wished to spare you the grief and sorrow I suffered. But my magic wand wasn't strong enough to alter your path.

Before long, one day you will clear the fog – lift the veil and see into your soul who you really are. When you do, you will stand in awe at your perfection - your beautiful, magnificent self. You will wonder what happened and why it took you so long to open your eyes to this undeniable truth. You will realize that you really are the creator of your world. And in all the chaos that's discarded around your feet like piles of dirty laundry, was only a disguise that you needed to wear to get through the hard part – the learning stages of the human experience.

You will realize that the costumes you wore of depression, anxiety, feeling alone, lost and forsaken were merely a part of the act…an intricate part of your divine plan for a standing ovation worthy performance. You will take a bow and acknowledge in you, a job well done.

When you see your reflection in your eyes you will see love. You will remember that you are love. And that you've always been loved. You will wonder what took you so long to see who you really are, Goddess Daughter…Keeper of the Children. Your strength is saving humanity. Your love is strengthening the new generation which is the foundation of our new world.

Thank you, Daughter for your bravery, your persistence and unwavering spark of hope and joy.

I love you,

The Universe

I sign the letter and ask Husband to do the same. My prayer is that Daughter will use these words as comfort when needing a dose of love, admiration and support for her magnificent self. I pray Daughter's path to self-love is shorter than mine.

Chapter 14

THE PHOENIX TAKES FLIGHT

I'm in Tumwater, Washington and Dad picks me up from the shuttle van drop-off point. We visit AuntM for a short time then head out for the drive to his home. Dad jerks the wheel to the left and avoids the Hyundai Elantra from sideswiping us in his white 2009 Nissan Altima. We stop short of the freeway entrance due to thick traffic. Bam! KaBam! Bam! We jolt forward into the rear of the car that nearly struck us seconds ago. Our bodies ricochet back and forth, our seatbelts keeping us from flying through the front window. My head snaps back against the headrest. The seatbelt locks me in but creates a sore spot under my right rib. Vomit threatens to spew any moment. We sit in shock, sandwiched between cars.

We spend our only two days together at the doctor and insurance offices. No broken bones. No blood. Dad is able to drive but I cannot see straight. I'm deeply grateful that Dad and I healed our wounds of the past and we are eager to be together. In ways, our time now reminds me of our devotion when I was a child. Ironically, this crash is only about a mile from where we lived when I was five. Back in the olden days of my running around the yard, carefree, doing my hula dance for him and Grandma.

So much pain and separation, both physical and emotional, has slipped between us. He was my idol, my first love and hero. And then life took twists and turns that neither of us expected and he fell off his pedestal. It's hard to explain, but this accident is actually a gift on many levels.

Dad is my hero again. I see the beautiful man he is. The man who always wanted to keep me safe, but didn't know how. The man who loved me more than any man ever will. The man who is driving us home, safe and sound after all we've been through. I am sad that our time is over and I must leave.

The plane ride home is long and I am eager to see Chiropractor. Why did this have to happen? My body is going through enough. Now I must deal with the fragility of my human form. Light touch is too much trauma but I must endure massages and spinal adjustments. My neck throbs and feels like it's on the verge of bending in half.

Chiropractor says I am healing quicker than most. I know this is because I use energy healing to clear the trauma. What surprises me is that this time, Husband is concerned about me after the accident. His voice is soft and caring, unlike 20 plus years ago. His love brings healing to me and I cry. He really does care about me.

******

JoyToTheWorld and I become fast friends. She is a powerful alchemist and we swap healing sessions. We are always here for each other, encouraging the other to fly higher. We know we are soul sisters and grateful to find each other.

Her healing magic digs deep into my heart, soul and inner children. The more soul we heal, the more hatred I release and transmute to love and forgiveness. My beautiful, strong, body, mind and spirt is shifting into a deeper love for myself. I'm grateful for her powers, for it takes a mighty goddess to help me down to my core.

She suggests that I might have post-traumatic stress disorder just like GoddessHealer thought. We focus on my nervous system which is still on constant high alert and ready for battle at a seconds notice. We recalibrate my limbic system and call it my new relaxation system. Nerves start settling down. Immune system is building and a deeper level of happiness is flowing into my life. What needs more healing at the core keeps spewing to the surface.

I'm waking up faster on a soul and spiritual level. Old emotional buttons get pushed and I recognize them as opportunities to transmute the sorrow to freedom rather than from a victim perspective. New friends filter towards me. I'm stepping into my greatness. Coming out from behind the curtain. Business is rapidly expanding, helping many others heal their crap just like I am doing in my life.

My tool box of energy healing techniques grows rapidly. Clients come to me to help them ease their pain. They report learning to love themselves, know that they matter, de-stress, and become conscience manifestors. These people are grateful for the tools I share that empower them on their journey to self-discovery.

Life is good. Life is expansive and I am grateful every day to be alive. It's okay for me to look at my past in awe and marvel at the beauty of it. Being alive no longer makes me sick.

**

Healing is sort of like a spider web. Start on the perimeter and work your way in to the center where all the threads connect. The core is the causative emotion caused by trauma. The ripple effect is how the fallout of the experience plays out over time. We all have multiple spider webs that need untangling.

I'm now grateful for the dis-ease in my body. It led me to what I was searching for…yearning for….love. Love of myself. Love of the universe. Love of my entire family. Coming from a state of love and grace allows me to see that everyone really is doing the best they can with the tools they know how to use. There is a path to love for each of us and it's only limited by the choices we make along the way.

**

Dreams fill my nights and I wake exhausted. Boarded up buses parked along the curb. Burning buildings, oceans and rain puddles. Baby slipping out of her car seat. Speeding cars that nearly run me over. Twin giant brown bears eager to shred and eat me but saved by a glass door. Shattered rocks with red gems hidden inside. Artichokes, crabs and smeared salad on the floor. Blood spattered on the walls. Villains hurting me. Spiral staircases. And a golden cat.

DreamReader meets with me over and over and interprets my dreams. We sit on the ledge by the ocean as waves crash before us. His brown eyes and confident voice assures me every time that I am not crazy. My dreams are not the literal movie that they portray. He expertly explains that what goes on in my head at night are all good. They show my growth and moving forward in life. This is another form of healing. Dreams are how my subconscious and conscious self are working in tandem to bring faster and faster relief. I'm forever grateful for DreamReader for understanding me, calming my fears and encouraging me to keep dreaming.

**

The cusp of Year of the Ram brings more expansion. GoddessHealer guides me through a massive healing session. First we do the usual relaxing through breathing and giving myself permission to let go of tension. Even though I've survived countless healing sessions, a twinge of apprehension knocks at the door of my left brain. So, like I do with my clients, GoddessHealer gently guides me into a state of trusting my higher self and the guidance of the universe.

She connects me to my inner child who is still stuck in time. My heart and soul release a torrent of hatred towards StepMom. I scream out at the witch that hexed my life. I hate this woman with every cell of my body and I wish I could kill her. Rage spews like an erupted sewer line flooding my home with stench and rot.

The urge to kill someone surprises a part of me yet feels natural. I vomit words that were stored for decades, stuffed into crevices of my soul and gut. Even the hatred towards Father wasn't as intense as it is for StepMom. My heart longs to kill her. Make her pay for what she did to me every day of my life since crossing the threshold of my childhood. Yes, if it was legal, I would kill her!

Purging, purging, purging. At last, tears dry and I breathe again. My heart and soul shift and within moments, I forgive StepMom for being so hateful to me. I now see her as a great teacher. She showed me how to be a better mother. I turned her loathing and intolerance of me into love for my children. What she did, I did the opposite. I'm surprisingly grateful for my experiences with her. I learned to stand my ground, see my value and beauty. To grow a spine and stand up to the one person who nearly destroyed me.

My body responds to this new level of peace. A touch of weight fills out on my bones. My immune system grows stronger. Physical and mental endurance builds. And then I am triggered and an urge to battle with StepMom resurfaces. Will I ever purge myself of her?

Still more healing gurgles up for clearing. I'm driven to purge every last infected cell of darkness. Nothing will stop me. I am tenacious when I want something bad enough. Rising above my past and fully stepping into emotional, physical and spiritual balance is my never ending goal.

This time, JoyToTheWorld steps in and we travel back to another lifetime on invisible waves. Past life regression is still pretty new to me but the process feels right. We've done this before with great healing success. The famous psychic, Sylvia Browne's book, *Past Lives, Future Healing,* and the ground breaking book, *Many Lives, Many Masters,* by psychiatrist Brian Weiss M.D. teaches about the power of making restitution from our past lives. The concept, before delving into actually experiencing it the first time, always intrigued me. And scared me a little. A part of me chuckles over how much I've changed. What used to feel scary, ungodly or insane is now normal. Before the session, I felt that more clearing needed to happen around my nemesis, StepMom.

We begin…

I eagerly pull back energetic curtains and find myself as a male tribe's person. Here I am, standing tall with dark skin, muscular arms and buff core. A loin cloth wraps around my waist. It appears that Step-Mom and I met a long time ago. In this past lifetime, she murdered my family. I see myself standing, on guard, ready to attack and slaughter the creature that stole my family. As I confront her, with my spear in right hand, I spew hatred and rage and call her a coward and a murderer. My heart is broken and I vow revenge. I order her to come out of hiding from behind the rock that she seeks for protection. I warn her I am going to kill her for taking away all that I love. Rage and hatred are all I feel towards her.

When given the chance to raise my spear and stab her to death, I pause. And refuse. My soul whispers that I am not a murderer. My heart says to forgive. And so, being the mighty warrior, I shift and choose the strength of forgiveness instead. An all knowing consumes me and tells me that violence is not me. Killing is not me. Not even taking revenge on the most horrendous person in my life.

Instead of seeing a wretched human hiding behind the rock, I see a tall beam of light that is her soul. Our souls speak. Through the process, I see the bigger picture. She was my teacher. Now I fully understand that my life lesson is forgiveness. My soul weeps. Rage and hatred dissipates and heals the holes of destruction as I tell StepMom that I love her. At last, I lay down my spear and release her. Let her go for all lifetimes. Including the one we are living right now. Forgiveness on the heart and soul level is what healing and transformation is all about.

**

Emotional triggers bring more healing. Buttons that used to cause bleeding in my colon now make me hungry for more releasing because I know healing is mine. I've climbed to the top of my highest jagged mountain peak and am now on the downhill slide. Faster and deeper the wounds mend and return to wholeness. Dr. Wayne Dyer says, "A change in thought is a change in destiny." My thoughts are rapidly changing and I'm eager for my new life ahead.

Another piece of my soul calls, telling me she is ready for attention. Again, JoyToTheWorld walks with me on my path to transformation. As I relax into our regression session, I find myself, once again, facing the truck accident from my children's youth.

Within moments, my soul screams a mournful cry that I will die today. I am spent with the burden and suffering of the human condition. Man wore me out. Won the battle against me. I welcome death as my savior. An instant before surrendering to the frozenness of the night, the soft whispers of infant Daughter and toddler Son call out to me on invisible waves. In unison they plead, "Please, Mommy, don't die. We need you."

Their love and innocence yanks me back from the point of no return and I vow to stay alive. For them. And to leave the binds of marriage as soon as Children are grown. Hatred towards Husband for his disregard to my living, disguised as shock and sorrow spew from my angry lips. I hate him for wishing me dead on that night. I hate him for loving a piece of steel and rubber more than *me.* I hate him for destroying a piece of me that will never be the same. My spark was nearly snuffed out.

A part of me is surprised that the accident still festers, buried at the bottom of the deepest crevices of my heart. Rage, grief, and despair pollute the air around me as I continue to purge. The releasing and wailing of decades-old chaos is almost too much to handle. My whole body wracks uncontrollably with wailing and oceans of tears.

As I vomit more torment from my bones, blood and flesh, the lens of my perspective begins to shift. My soul starts to see that he did the best he could. I recognize that his cold heartedness towards me was perhaps his way of coping. His way of masking the fear that he nearly became a widower and single father of a three-year-old and one-year-old. I don't know for sure if this is true but it's what I choose to believe. My heart softens and I forgive him for his inability to express love the way I needed it. I forgive myself for harboring hate for so many years. For letting man nearly take me down completely.

As I come back to present time, I ponder the depth of that tragedy. It not only ruined my marriage but I came within breaths of dying for real. My soul fragmented that day and a big part stayed in a coma all these years. But she is fully awake now. I feel her coming to life and growing stronger by the moment. Her lungs fill with possibilities and sparks of hope. She is ready to live every day with gusto. With love. Forgiveness. With my soul no longer fragmented, I welcome more healing and expansion along the way.

I'm grateful to myself for listening to the calling of Son and Daughter. Had I tuned them out, they would have grown up not knowing how much I love them. How I lived for them. How I would die without them. They would morph into adults not knowing who I am. Because of them. I avoided being a statistic. Another fatality of a freezing winter night on a slippery I-80 highway. Thankfully, because of them, I live long enough to show them who I am. Because of them, I grew as a mother and a friend. Son and daughter were the perfect balance…Son in his steady strength, ready to hold my hand when I needed a lift…his quiet, gentle spirit giving me peace in the storm. Daughter in her spunk showing me that I am only love and challenging me to step further away from the controlling parenting style of my childhood. Together they even the scales, reminding me of the gifts of life.

What I've learned through this healing journey is that forgiveness and love are what matter most. Every player in my version of the game of life was integral in helping me seek my truth. They pushed me to see my strength and that I matter. They forced me to stand up for myself and declare my right to happiness in this chaotic world. Without them, life would be monotone. With them, it's filled with every color on the spectrum.

Some say that healing is like peeling an onion. Or is it more like carving a statue? Chip, chip, chip away at the hard, unassuming exterior. The self-healer is the master craftsman creating a masterpiece, one whack of the chisel at a time, until the final figure is complete. Sometimes needing to go back and chip away more at spots that previously seemed perfect. Add buffing and polishing to coax out even more brilliance. This takes time and effort and is worth striving for. As a result of years of racing to the finish line, willing myself to heal, I notice remarkable changes inside and out. Gone are the days of drinking myself numb or stuffing my gut with the false promise of everlasting love from a sugar induced high. Gone are the days of being responsible for everyone else's happiness but my own. No more loathing myself as I pass a mirror or see my reflection in a store window. I've become my own best friend. And this feels right. My gut is no longer a storage unit for rage and hatred because those toxins are now purged and replaced with joy, zest for living and deep gratitude.

I'm forever grateful to Dad for bravely adopting me. Doing everything he could in the beginning to claim me as his daughter. Then keeping me with him the best he could, throughout his own battles. Being a single parent to an energetic child in the early years is no easy feat. He loved me when others couldn't.

He taught me to be independent, to comb my hair and instilled good work ethics. I love him with my whole heart and soul. He was my anchor. Even now, I'd be lost without him. He is my first love. He was and is always proud of me. I just couldn't see it as a little girl because I felt so broken and unlovable the way I was. I'm proud of Dad too and grateful that he is mine. I love him with my whole heart and soul.

I'm grateful for being put up for adoption and raised in America, the land that others only dream of experiencing. Life was not easy for Mother and Father and I know they did what was best. Being born and living in Hawaii is something that others only fantasize about too. This makes me realize that other people's dreams are my reality.

Mother and I have a unique friendship and my heart has only love for her. We will never have the traditional mother-daughter bond because she wasn't there to kiss my skinned knees or dry tears from my eyes. But that's okay. We have a connection that is tender, supportive and free. She is one of my biggest supporters, always encouraging me to fly higher. Be all I can be.

As I sit and ponder what her life must have been like, softness crosses my heart. As one mother to another, I cannot even begin to fathom the anguish she must have endured giving birth to me, feeling alone, and then against her will, hand me over to someone else to rear. A tightness squeezes my throat as I put myself in her position, and I confess that I'd never have the strength to do what she did out of love and survival for me. I make peace with her, right now, and allow the backlog of her love that I resisted all these years begin to flow and cradle my heart and soul. My inner baby. Her energy rocks me back and forth, close to her bosom, assuring me that I was wanted all along. I can relax now.

Father's genuine love for me radiates through the phone lines. His heart touches mine as if there is no separation in distance. We don't need to say much to the other, we just "know", with every cell of our body, that all is well between us. We are so much alike.

I'm grateful for StepMom for loving me the only way she knew how. I see her fears and insecurities and want her to know that I love her with all my heart. I will always be grateful for the times she stood up for me. As a healed adult, I see that she was only a child herself, raising someone else's child. StepMom was twelve years older than me when she stepped into the daunting role as my mother. Most of all, I'm grateful that she taught me the lesson of forgiveness which is priceless.

I'm grateful to Husband for giving me the only safe and stable home I'd ever known. And for the most beautiful gifts of children a mother could hope for. I'm humbled by his ability to be stoic and stick with me through my internal torment that plagued me every day of our marriage. I will love him forever.

I'm grateful for the parade of healers who walked this healing journey with me. Without them, I would not be here. Especially GoddessHealer and JoyToTheWorld.

I'm grateful for BestFriend in Utah who always encouraged me to keep flying and never let me crash. And Sister for always being by my side even when great distance separated us. She taught me how to do puzzles, encouraged my mischievous side and loved me like only a big sister can.

Grandma, even though I cannot see her in physical form, is with me every moment of every day. She is in the birds that sing, sunsets on the ocean and the salt laced wind that kisses me daily. She sleeps with me, comforts me and fills my heart with unconditional love.

I am grateful for StepGrandad and StepGrandma. They took me in and considered me one of their own. Even though my inner child was angry at times, I forgive myself for not understanding life on the adult level back then. They gave us a home. Twice. StepGrandma even taught me her secret to even better pie crust than Grandma's. Milk. Not water. Both Grandmothers infused my life with other secret ingredients. Not only through baking, but life in general. Love. Strength. Wisdom.

My belief is that I endured the deep level of suffering in this lifetime in order to expand my soul and help people. Because of this journey of self-discovery, self-healing, and years of being a student and client, learning and absorbing all I could about healing and energy, I do help people. I know I am blessed and honored to help others do what I have done. My prayer is that those who come to me experience great love, joy, peace and freedom.

When those with broken hearts, wounded inner children and aching or dying souls come to me, I honestly say, "I know how you feel."

And they recognize this truth. I assure them that their pain will pass and that the process of releasing their old crap will be worth it.

People tell me that they are drawn in by my energy. I assure them that they can have what I have if they really want it. And I'll hold their hand along the way if they choose. Together we work and play, using the magic of energy healing and coaching to transform their life.

A healer explained that people like me stop family patterns through the ancestral line and have the hardest life. Well, I recognize that is me. I stopped the pattern of child abuse. I stopped infant daughters from being cast out of the family system. Mother was not the first to hand over a baby. GreatGrandmother gave away several and walked out on two, never looking back. One of the daughters she abandoned was Mother. The other was NewMother.

My desire is to be a beacon of hope, like a lighthouse in the storm. It's important that those who seek healing must know to *never give up!* Healing is a bumpy ride and well worth the tears, time and effort. The darkness before the light can seem overwhelming. But hang on! Life will get better…so long as you let it. Keep riding the waves.

I'm grateful for all my experiences and welcome the peace that I've earned. Growing up, I never saw myself as competitive. But now I realize that I really am. I compete with myself. Therefore I am guaranteed to win provided I never give up. And I never have nor will I ever. Now I can honestly say that I not only survived, but I thrive. I've given myself the gift of life, happiness and sanity.

The greatest gift of all though is freedom and finally knowing who I am…

Chapter 15

I AM

I Am the morning dew that kisses the green grass, awakening her to another glorious day. My moisture drips down to the dry soil, eagerly awakening her to her full beauty.

I Am bouquets of purple and white lilacs that tickle the noses of those who pause a moment and take in my perfume. Their deep breaths drink in my softness and fill their lungs with moments of peace.

I Am Orange cream sickle and root beer floats. The froth from the sweet ice cream fizzing in mouths making giggles like a four-year-old on a warm summer day. Laughter that crosses lips sends bouncing wave lengths of joy to the universe.

I Am the breeze that cools the weary traveler bringing relief and lending him strength to carry on his way.

My life glistens with gold and silver and rainbow shades of blue, purple and red.

I Am a crocheted blanket to those whose hearts are frozen from fear, anger and abandonment. My love weaves the stitches of warmth on a cold winter day. My yarn provides love and the comfort of knowing they have a safe place to rest. As I wrap them in my embrace, I send them messages that they are safe and loved. I remind them that they are never alone.

I Am one with the Universe. With mankind.

I Am peace in the storm. Those who know me come to me for strength and encouragement to ride out the wind. Holding their hand in mine as they wade the waters to the open field of their dreams.

I Am love in the heart of those who feel unloved. Unworthy. Like a mistake. For I know who they are and see inside them, their brilliance that one day soon, they too will discover.

I Am healing in the soul that reconnects the weary with themselves after a lifetime of chaos of the third dimension.

I Am a part of God – the Universe. I am one with All That Is. I am healed and I am here to help others do the same. I am on purpose. With a purpose.

I Am gratitude for all the lessons and growth that comes from pain and suffering.

No longer are the days of me questioning who I Am. Long gone are the days of doubting myself, hating myself, wanting to die. No more days of confusion, torment and rage.

For I never was those things. They were simply masks that I wore in this lifetime disguising who I really am. No more being a hypocrite, wearing costumes that hide my Light …hiding in the darkness and safety behind the curtain. No more façade of being small, when in fact I am great.

My life looks like the morning sun reflecting off the ocean, casting beams of heat, passion and wonder.

My life smells like cinnamon, roses, and plumeria. And tastes like warm, homemade peach pie with a scoop of vanilla ice cream on top. My life sounds like laughter, ocean waves lapping at the sandy shore, singing birds and geckos chirping confirmation that this is true.

I Am a transmitter of love, of peace. Of Joy.

I Am a reminder that every person is indeed beautiful and perfect and what they see in me is simply a reflection of what's inside them. For they too are all of these things, and more.

Most of all…*I Am…Alive!*

Are You Tired of the Pain and Ready to Heal Your Soul?

Dear friend, I lovingly ask, "What's hurting deep inside you?" What is your soul crying out, yearning to finally heal? Does your heart still feel broken, shattered and closed off from betrayal and rejection? When you stop and look within, what do you see? What do you feel? Is your inner child crying out for love and approval? What part of your past is still haunting you?

Letting go of the pain and beginning to heal starts with awareness. Waking up and realizing that old patterns and behaviors no longer serve your highest good might be a process. Or it might smack you up alongside the head and shout, "Wake up now!"

The next step is having the desire to let go of your old story and create a new one. Be honest here. Are you tired from silently sabotaging yourself? Are you ready to stop the dis-ease of suffering? Are you ready to shed the numbness that still protects you?

Are you ready to take charge of your life and finally feel ALIVE? What you do with the trauma of your past is up to you. You don't have to go through another day harboring grief, anger, sadness or being powerless. In fact, did you know that it's your birthright to live happily deep down to your core...for your soul to sing, expand and be unstoppable? To know, without a doubt, that you are loved. Special. Worthy. Feel safe...And be free from the invisible chains that keep you captive?

How will your life be different once you stop feeling abandoned and alone...reverse the erosion that eats away at your self- worth and instead, stand in confidence...own your truth that you are wanted and powerful?

Before going any further, hear this: I'm sorry for the pain and suffering you lived through. What happened to you, regardless of the ugly details, was not okay. However, it's important that you understand that how and what you did to survive was and is valid. You did the best you could. In fact, you are still doing the best you can in this moment. Thank you for being who you are. Thank you for still being here. You matter.

When you stay in a pain state, you keep reliving the past. Face it, what is done is done. You survived and now you have the choice to learn the lessons from your experiences, move on and thrive or stay stuck. Your beautiful, expansive future is waiting for you. Transformation through mending your heart and soul takes action. Own the fact that you are in charge of your life and don't have to be a victim anymore.

Is now the right time for you to speak up, break free and reclaim your power? Is now the time for you to shed the masks that keep the real you hidden? Is now the time to open up and realize that you deserve your deepest hearts desires...step into freedom from the exhaustion of emotional turmoil...declare that YOU are special...and stop stuffing and lugging around the pain?

If now is not the right time for you to step out, heal your soul, transform and stop what's hurting, then when is?

The right time for me to stop the pain is _______________________

Reaching out for help is scary. I know that you are brave though. How do I know this? Because you read my story. This is a great start. You were brave enough to stick with me till the end…even through the parts that made you feel uncomfortable. That took real courage. What made you feel uncomfortable made me uncomfortable too but you hung in there.

People ask me how I healed, saved and transformed my life. My blueprint is available to anyone, including you. What I did first was identify and admit that I had a big problem and own my truth that I had the power to resolve it. The next step was the desire to heal. That started with being open to letting go of my ego and surrendering to the calling of my soul. Making the decision to use unconventional (by Western standards) means to save myself was scary but I picked up the phone and dialed for help anyway. I was ready and willing to take the wrath of anyone who thought I was nuts to use "wacky" ways to heal.

Persistent action was one of my saving graces. I never gave up even though I wanted to more times than I can count. After years of learning and using different healing methods, the real magic happened once I began to forgive, become grateful for all that happened and love myself. That's when real freedom swooped in and took me to new heights. My soul became free to be me.

A vital part of the forgiveness process was healing my wounded inner child that was stuck in a time warp, reliving traumatic events as if they were still occurring in present time. We create aspects that make us constantly abuse ourselves and they need healing too.

Clearing ancestral trauma that was brought forward in my DNA and bringing forgiveness to my genetic line was important.

Removing negative energetic attachments that kept me stuck and in darkness was huge. Letting go of other people's limiting beliefs about me, themselves, God, the ability to self-heal and life freed me so I could live by my beliefs. My truths. For me, bringing forth and forgiving transgressions from past lives was vital. My soul wanted the "full meal deal" experience of healing.

Not everyone needs to take the expansive journey that was my soul's agenda. But everyone can benefit from at least some of my path. Take what you need and leave the rest. If nothing else, stay open and brave and set the intention that you receive what you need.

We all have the power to heal. That includes you. You feel the spark of hope, don't you!? My hope is your hope. My strength is your strength. Lean on me if that helps. You saw what happens when you let go, trust and believe in yourself and never, ever give up. You heard how magnificent life is when you step into who you really are. You lived the gifts of gratitude.

Take a few moments and check in with yourself. Breathe and center your energy with all of your focus on your heart. Ask these questions and fill in your answers:

1. My biggest take-away or ah ha's from this story that apply to me are:

2. I recognize that I am still holding a grudge/resentment/anger towards:

3. The areas of my life that feel out of balance, out of control or hurt are:

4. What area of my life am I ready, willing, eager and able to take charge of and change for the better?

   Work

   Relationships

   Health

   Other

5. What am I tired of tolerating?

6. What is the best way for me to start the process of letting go?

> Read more books
> Make a phone call
> Send an email
> Look within myself, my past, present and future on a deeper level
> Other

What comes next?

Forgiveness, Gratitude, Love, and real Freedom.

Like you read through the story, you saw that it is possible to drastically change your life. You witnessed how it's possible to forgive someone who ripped out your heart and nearly destroyed you to the core. You experienced how freeing life is once you clear out the chaos, love yourself and live your biggest dream. You now understand that you too are in charge of your happiness.

If you apply the basic principles of forgiveness towards those who betrayed you, gratitude and acknowledgement for the lessons learned and expand your heart to love, you too will heal your life and be FREE…regardless of the chaos around you.

I encourage you to contact me and let me know how my story helped you. More importantly though, tell me about your challenges, your obstacles, what's hurting you and what you're tired of tolerating. In fact, if you would like, we can set up a complementary consultation, no obligation, by phone or video chat and see how I might be able to help you. It doesn't matter where you live. If I can't help you, I promise to be honest.

My email address is info@align-with-joy.com and my cell is 1-808-

268-2407. If you prefer, you can text me with your name and time zone. Either way, we'll schedule your complimentary consultation. Distance is not an issue because people reach out to me in the USA and beyond. Maybe I'm the right person to help you on a deeper level, maybe I'm not but there is only one sure way to find out. I don't have all the answers but will do my best to guild you to what you need.

Thank you from the depths of my heart for allowing me to be a part of your life, even if for only a little while. My wish for you is that you always remember that you are loved, that you matter, hang on to hope…and never give up!

In love and gratitude,

Wendy Lee Baldwin

P.S. Keep reading! The following pages include powerful tools to help you start letting go of what's hurting and start healing your soul and transforming your life today. This is your **Secret Formula to Your Best Life Ever... Forgiveness + Gratitude + Love = FREEDOM!**

Do this:

1. Get out your pen

2. Sit quietly and uninterrupted

3. Take a moment and center yourself. Do this by closing your eyes, take in a few deep breaths in and out while calling back all of your energy. Call your energy back from your family, work, the commute home, store clerks and anyone else you crossed paths with. You will notice that you will start to feel stronger and more centered. Always remember to breathe!

"Forgiving does not erase the bitter past.
A healed memory is not a deleted memory.
Instead, forgiving what we cannot forget
creates a new way to remember.
We change the memory of our past into a hope for our future."

— Lewis B. Smedes,

Chapter 16

FORMULA FOR FORGIVENESS

Disclaimer: By implementing the ideas, suggestions and questions throughout this material, you understand and agree that using the following material is experiential and used at your own risk. Following the strategies in this handout/printout/package are not approved by the FDA or reviewed by a licensed medical doctor or psychiatric professional. Do NOT use the information in this package if you are heavily medicated with legally prescribed psychotropic drugs and/or have a history of a mental disorder, without the written consent of your medical provider. You release Wendy Baldwin, Wendy Lee Baldwin, Align With Joy and anyone associated from any harm or liability.

FORGIVENESS...
HEALING YOUR HEART and SOUL

Forgiveness:

→ The act of releasing the negative emotional charge as a result of someone hurting you. Letting go of grudges. Freeing self of emotional burdens toward another person.

→ Three reasons why this is important:

1. You will no longer be a prisoner of your past

2. Ultimate healing and transformation on the heart and soul level

3. You reclaim your power!

The Offenders

Give yourself permission to sit quietly, close your eyes, and relax. Take a couple deep breaths in through your nose and out through your mouth. Let go of the tension in your body and acknowledge your courage in answering the following questions. Be honest and as complete as possible.

If you start to feel upset while doing these exercises, give yourself permission to acknowledge your emotions. Part of the healing process is understanding what you feel that's buried deep inside. Write out your answers below.

1. Who hurt me? Their names are…

2. What they did to me…

3. How did I react to their thoughtless, reckless treatment towards me?

4. How is this continuing to affect my life?

5. How many years have these events impacted my life in some way and caused me pain?

6. Who have I treated wrongly?

7. What did I do that was wrong or hurtful?

8. How many years have I dragged around this guilt?

9. Am I ready, willing and eager to let go and forgive those who have hurt me?

10. Am I ready, willing and eager to let go of the pain that I caused someone?

11. If not now, when is a good time to do so?

"Forgiveness is not always easy. At times, it feels more painful than the wound we suffered to forgive the one that inflicted it. And yet, there is no peace without forgiveness."

— Unknown

Stuck Letting Go?

Holding onto grudges can feel "good" for only so long. If you don't let go and forgive, then you're stuck with more of the same pain, different day.

Did you know that holding onto the pain is only hurting you? The other person is NOT the one suffering. You are!!

Also, you might not like hearing this, but refusing to let go of suffering has what is called a Secondary Gain. This means you are subconsciously benefiting from staying stuck.

Common examples:

- Being in a pain state is a part of your identity. You are seen as a victim and that makes people give you more empathy
- You don't know who you are or will be without the hurt and blaming others because it's all you know

If you find yourself not wanting to let go and forgive, take time and explore the following angles:

1.   How will my life improve once I let go and forgive?

2.   Who will I be once I let go and forgive?

3.   How will my life heal and expand?

4.   What is the #1 benefit of not forgiving?

5.   If now is not the right time to forgive, when will the time be right?

Important note: It's okay if you aren't ready to fully forgive those who hurt you. That will come as you heal. Give yourself permission to be where you are in your journey. Be okay that you are in the process of forgiveness. Be gentle on yourself. It's okay to say, "I'm in the process of forgiving…"

Letting Go

Here is a formula for helping you start letting go and shifting into a state of forgiveness:

1.   Sit quietly with yourself. Close your eyes. Take a few deep breaths in through your nose and exhale out through your mouth. Call all of your energy back to you. Your energy gets scattered throughout the day. Call your energy back from work, family, anyone you encountered while driving, shopping or any other interactions with people.

2. If possible, play relaxing, healing music in the background. This is not necessary but might be helpful.

   You might also wish to call in the energy of God/Universe/ Source/Angels to surround and support you (if this is within your belief system.)

3. Call forward the energy of the offender. Either see or feel their image/presence. Say out loud…

   "I give myself permission to release ____________ (insert name) from the obligation of making me happy, feel worthy or whole.

   I choose to release the anger, and hurt that is attached to this.

   I choose, right now, to forgive you – for my sake – and set us both free.

   Thank you for the lessons learned."

4. Say Ho'Oponopono prayer out loud. This is a powerful prayer used by the Hawaiian's and other Pacific Islanders. Do not let the simplicity fool you. The words and meaning are powerful! You can use the phrases in any order.

"I'm sorry"
"Please forgive me"
"I love you"
"Thank you"

NOTE: When you start off, you might not feel "sorry" or want to ask for "forgiveness." That's okay. Trust your higher self to take over and you will begin to shift.

Also, when reciting the prayer, you might find it helpful to direct this at the offender and then to yourself and the situation at large. Once you've sent out the prayer at least a few times, take a few cleansing breaths and get ready for the next step.

1. Continue holding the energy/vision of the offender. Start talking to this person as if he/she is in the room with you. The person will not be allowed to "speak". *Only listen.* Express out loud everything this person needs to hear that you never got to say.

2. Pretend to see or feel that you are connecting heart to heart, soul to soul with this person. Listen to what comes to you.

3. If the person is too horrible, and you don't want to connect on the heart and soul level, do what feels right to come to some level of resolution. Do you need to see the person shrink or vanish? Then in your mind's eye, make them do just that.

4. Pretend to see/feel the energetic connection between you and the other person let go. You might cut a cord that tethers you together, let a balloon carry the connections away or any other process that assists in the letting go process. The important part is witnessing and acknowledging the release.

5. If the offender is too mean, scary or intimidating, then see/feel yourself surrounded by your personal support system. This can be family, God/Angels/Guides, friends…whatever feels safe and secure to you.

Note: You are never alone in the healing process!

Next Step

Here's a secret…The most important person to forgive is yourself.

*"You will begin to heal when you let go of past hurts,
forgive those who have wronged you and
learned to forgive yourself for your mistakes."*

— Unknown

1. Look back on yourself at the age you were when the offender hurt you. Notice how you were at that time. Allow yourself to see that you were doing the best you could under the circumstances.

2. Give the current you permission to forgive the younger you. Send your younger self lots of love and gratitude. It's safe to cry! Notice that you did NOTHING wrong. Let go of the anger, fear and self-doubt.

3. This is a good time to rewrite the script and make something positive from what used to be negative. Ask your soul what she/he learned from the past experience.

4. Look yourself in the mirror and acknowledge that you are doing the best you can. And that you are INCREDIBLE. BRAVE. BEAUTIFUL!

Lessons Through Forgiveness

*"True forgiveness is when you can say,
"Thank you for that experience."*

— Oprah Winfrey

A part of the forgiveness process is shifting the lens from the victim perspective to the soul's agenda. When you do this, you see the lessons that the experience gave you. Embrace them and expand your wisdom. Ask, "What positive lessons did I and my soul learn about myself as a result of the trauma between me and the other person?" For example:

- Did I learn that the offender and I actually had a misunderstanding, and therefore, the value of communication is now clear?
- Did I learn how strong I am?
- Did I learn to stand up for myself?
- Did I learn to be more discerning of other people and situations?
- Did I learn to trust myself more?

Side note: Sometimes the suffering and lessons of your past opens doors to your life purpose. Maybe what you learned is that you have a mission to help others who have gone through similar experiences. What if your traumatic past is a foundation for you becoming the beacon of hope for abused women or children?

1. List and expand on as many positive life lessons you learned.

2. What have I learned about myself through this forgiveness process?

> *"Forgiveness is unlocking the door to set someone free and…*
> *realizing you were the prisoner!"*
>
> — Max Lucado

Now, go give yourself a giant, well-deserved hug.

Chapter 17

FORMULA FOR GRATITUDE

"Gratitude is the sign of noble souls."

— Aesop

Gratitude is one of **the biggest secrets in life!** Gratitude is like a magic potion that helps you feel happier and get more of what you desire. The vibration of gratitude will:

- Change yours or someone else's sour mood to sweet
- Bring you more of what you DO desire
- Soften a hardened heart
- And makes you more likeable!

Seriously! Who are you more willing to help and be thoughtful towards? Someone who is grateful or someone who doesn't acknowledge you?

Since you and everything around you is energy, the high vibration of gratitude will bring you more high vibrational experiences and people.

237

Important note: It's okay if you aren't ready to be grateful for those who hurt you. That will come as you heal. Give yourself permission to be where you are in your journey. Be okay that you are in the process of being grateful.

Use the space here to write out what you are grateful for. Be sure and include new insights. For example, any life lessons that were painful but informative and helped you grow. Include family, friends, home…anything that comes from your heart.

I'm grateful for:

How are you willing to start including more gratitude in your daily life? List your thoughts here.

1.

2.

3.

Who are three people that would benefit from hearing the heartfelt words, "Thank you," from you?

1.

2.

3.

Make a point, right now to let them know how they made your life better. See what happens!

Being Grateful For Me

When was the last time you thanked YOURSELF?

You accomplish amazing feats all the time! Acknowledge yourself for this. For starters:

- You take care of other people

- You are important to all the people who love you – you matter

- You give others a reason to smile, feel loved and encourage them to be happy

Look at your magnificent, brilliant, beautiful body. Take a moment right now and thank your amazing:

- Digestive system

- back

- neck

- feet

- and every other part of your anatomy

Thank your body even if you are in physical pain. Did you know that the pain is telling you something? The discomfort is saying that it's time to *pay attention* to an area in your life that is out of balance. Be grateful for this. You have the power to change this. Your body will love you for it!

> *"The miracle of gratitude is that it shifts your perception to such an extent that it changes the world you see."*
>
> — Dr. Robert Holden

Write out a letter of gratitude to yourself:

Stand in front of the mirror. Look yourself in the eyes the best you can. And say, Thank you, thank you, thank you! Thank yourself for NEVER giving up!

Keep at the gratitude, and notice how your life begins to transform.

Chapter 18

FORMULA FOR LOVE

"You have to love yourself because no amount of love from others is sufficient to fill the yearning that your soul requires from you."

— Dodinsky

It's time to fall in love with your magnificent self! What was your response to that statement?

_____YIKES! That's scary...

_____I'm not lovable so why should I even try loving myself?

_____Hmmmm, seriously? Maybe....

_____YES! I'm ready! Bring on the lovefest!

THE most important relationship you will ever have in your life is the one you have with yourself. When you don't like or love yourself...hold onto anger (pure poison) all other relationships suffer. Become complicated, chaotic, and unfulfilling.

Use the following questions and exercises to dig deep and find your true, authentic self. Your true essence is buried beneath a lifetime of lies and deception. Lies from other people that you bought into for survival.

As the saying goes, truth will set you free. The truth is, you are a beautiful Being, worthy of the most magnificent love of all…Yours. On a scale of 0 – 10 with 0 = Not At All and 10= Absolutely!, how do you rate your level of self-love? _________

1. Your childhood story: Beliefs you picked up about yourself from siblings, parents, teachers, other kids, religion and others:

2. What was your relationship like with your father or father figure? Write out as clear of a picture as possible.

3. What was your relationship like with your mother or mother figure? Write out as clear of a picture as possible.

4. How have the relationships with your mother and father affected you in regards to your relationship with yourself?

    For example: Do you feel good or bad about yourself? Expand on these feelings.

5. What negative beliefs and behaviors, which you picked up from others, have you carried for a long time that hurt your relationship with yourself?

    For example: I'm stupid, fat, dumb, never amount to anything, a screw-up. I don't deserve a good life. I sabotage myself by:

6) Which of these beliefs and behaviors are working in your favor?

7) Which of these beliefs and behaviors are NOT working in your favor?

8) Are you ready, willing and eager to let go of all dysfunctional beliefs and behaviors towards yourself that you picked up from others?

9) If yes, you are ready, willing and eager to let go of all dysfunctional beliefs and behaviors towards yourself…what are your next steps? For example:

- Are you willing to forgive others?

- Forgive yourself for accepting their negative opinions of you?

- Forgive yourself for believing that you are anything less than magnificent?

- Take back your power?

- Start treating yourself like a best friend instead of someone you loathe?

- Are you ready to:

- Call someone for help?

- Invest in yourself?

- Be on a mission and do whatever it takes to step into self-love because at least a spark of you recognizes the truth that you deserve love and are loveable?

10. If you are not ready, willing and eager to let go of pain and start loving yourself…what's the benefit of staying stuck in the old patterns that block you from truly loving yourself?

11. When would be a good time to let go and start loving yourself on a deeper level?

12. Write out trauma around the relationship you have with yourself. For example, did/do you turn to drugs, alcohol, binging/purging, cutting, excessive shopping or any other self-destructive behaviors to subconsciously "punish" yourself or numb yourself?

13. Did/do any of these behaviors actually connect you to "feeling something" even if it's pain? If yes, expand on this the best you can.

Acknowledgement – Me to You

I acknowledge that something bad happened in your life. Perhaps more than once. Someone betrayed you on the deepest level and stole your trust and confidence. What happened to you is not okay. I'm sorry for the pain and suffering you've endure. Even though we don't know each other, know that I am proud of you.

I'm proud that you have the courage to look within and take these first steps towards healing and freedom. You are brave, strong and magnificent!

Acknowledgement – You to Yourself

A part of stepping into self-love is acknowledging yourself. You survived a lot of hardships. You also accomplished many amazing feats. You were courageous when life turned tough. You stood strong and did the best you could.

Take time and write out an acknowledgment to yourself. Be sure and include the hard times as well as the greatness that you were never given proper recognition for.

When finished writing, look in the mirror and read your acknowledgement out loud.

I acknowledge….

Formula For Love Part 2:

OPENING UP TO SELF LOVE

"You've been criticizing yourself for years and it hasn't worked. Try approving of yourself and see what happens."

— Louise Hay

Everything grows up and out from love. Another way of looking at it is, when you love yourself, you create balance and inner peace. It's time to become your own best friend.

1. What positive beliefs and behaviors do you seek to incorporate into your relationship with yourself?

2. If your best friend treated you the way you treat yourself, and thought of you in the same way that you believe about yourself, would this person still be your best friend?

_____Yes

_____No

3. List what needs to change so that you start becoming your own best friend:

4. What is the first step you plan to take in order to start treating yourself in a more positive way?

5. How will your life change when you start loving yourself?

6. How do you notice yourself blocking love? Do you:

   - Shrink back and reject compliments from others

   - Call yourself degrading/hurtful names

   - Avoid looking at yourself in the mirror, shop windows or cringe when someone takes your picture

   - Hide behind baggy, unattractive clothing

   - Or some other way….

7. If you notice resistance allowing love into your heart, acknowledge how you are feeling. Give yourself permission to feel this way. Then tell your ego to step aside and allow your higher self to take over.

   Close your eyes and BREATHE IN LOVE. Pretend to see love in front of you. Give it a shape, color and feeling. Now slowly take in a breath. And another one. Do this at least three times.

   Invite love in from the Universe/God/Source. Allow their love to flow down from the top of your head and into your heart. Put your hand on your heart to anchor it in. Do this for at least one minute.

   Keep practicing letting love in and it will get easier…When you love yourself, it's as if everything falls into place like magic!

"Love yourself enough to take actions required for your happiness… love yourself enough to cut yourself loose from the ties of the drama-filled past…love yourself enough to move on!"

— Dr. Steve Maraboli

Bonus challenge:

Did you know that being in a state of constant stress is an act of NOT loving yourself? Science proves that stress is addicting. The ongoing state of dis-ease eats away at you and can make you sick over the long haul. This happens because it creates inflammation in your body, drains your energy and throws your system out of whack. Your body is created to be in balance. In a state of ease.

One of the greatest acts of self-love you can give yourself is to destress. Challenge yourself to start implementing the following changes right away:

1. Stop taking on everyone else's problems. You are not in charge of them even if you think you are

2. Stop putting everyone else before you

3. Start making time, even if it's only 15 min a day, to nurture yourself

I will be blunt here. If you refuse to take a good hard look at this area of your life, then you are letting your ego be in charge. Not your heart, soul and higher self.

Keep this simple and start with one change. Then add another one. Keep building on small changes and before you know it, you'll have massive transformation.

Breathe!

Smile at yourself!

You are beautiful & magnificent!!

Chapter 19

FORMULA FOR FREEDOM

*"The secret to happiness is freedom.
The secret of freedom is courage."*

— Saul Alinsky

Freedom is what every heart and soul yearns for. Wars are fought for the right to be free. You don't have to fight. You have the right to be free, right now. Claim it!

Real freedom comes when you let go of the pain and suffering. Real freedom comes when you forgive, live in a state of gratitude and love yourself. Real freedom comes from transforming and designing your new life.

Use the following Release Form to help you let go even more.

- Fill in the person's name that hurt you
- Fill in the details
- Sign

Releasing the Past Official Document

My name: Date:

This is official notice to (person who hurt me) __________________
__________________. As of the date indicated above, by the official power invested in me, I release you from the following offenses:

1.

2.

3.

4.

I also release you from making me feel:

1.

2.

3.

4.

5.

In addition, I release you from the following belief systems that do not serve my highest good.

1.

2.

3.

4.

5.

I am done carrying these heavy, destructive emotions, beliefs and memories. I declare that by me signing this document, I give up the obligation of making you happy. Instead, I choose to be free and make myself happy, from this day forward.

I also choose to release you from the obligation or expectation of making me happy. I'm fully in charge of my happiness now.

I choose to live by my beliefs, expectations of myself and not yours or anyone else's.

I'm grateful, or in the process of being grateful, for the lessons I learned about myself, life and the benefits of my soul's expansion. By signing this document, I officially claim ownership of my entire life. I am now FREE!

Signature ____

Start Dreaming BIG!

*"Sometimes the way to personal freedom seems scary.
Take the first step and begin the release of doubt and fear.
Each new step builds confidence. Breathe. Don't look back."*

— Sheila Burke

Now the real fun starts!

Write out your new story. This is the vision of your life once you've purged old toxic emotions and step into forgiveness, gratitude and love.

Invoke the imagination of your inner child and start flushing out what freedom is to you. Play around with this. Relax and have fun!

1. My life sounds like:

2. My life smells like:

3. My life looks like:
4. My life tastes like:

5. My life feels like:

Use the space below and start writing out your own version of....

I Am

"Always remember that you are special,
that you are loved and that you matter.
Never give up on yourself because you are worth fighting for.
Let your light shine and live the rest of your life with gusto!"

— Wendy Lee Baldwin

ABOUT THE AUTHOR

Wendy Baldwin is a holistic/energy healer, Certified Wellness Coach, Certified Master Spiritual Coach, and Keynote Speaker. She mentors people who have been betrayed, broken hearted, abandoned, feel stuck, stressed out, overwhelmed and struggling with self-worth. She has helped a contless amount of people let go of their pain and suffering and transform, taking life to a higher level.

She also guides people along their path to reaching their goals, dreams and desires. Whether their ambition is through better health and wellness, expanding personal growth or reaching an "impossible" accomplishment, Wendy empowers everyone along the way. She supports the belief that successful people work with coaches and mentors.

Wendy understands and acknowledges the courage that it takes to reach out and ask for help. She understands pain, feeling broken on the deepest level and living in a state of detachment and numbness. She also understands defying other people's limiting beliefs and dreaming big.

Wendy is renowned for holding a safe, loving, non-judgmental space for people to share their deepest, darkest secrets. Her gentle spirit puts everyone at ease and fills them with a knowing that they are loved. Clients rave and glow at how she helped them change their life for the better.

Since the fourth grade, Wendy believed that God would not give us a dis-ease that we could not heal. Holding on to her belief, sometimes by a thread, helped her heal her life. Along the way, she learned priceless skills and picked up powerful tools that she uses to help others get out of the chaos and reclaim their power. Her extensive training and experiences afford her the insights and knowledge to help others clear their crap faster and live the expansive, fulfilling life they deserve.

Wendy aims to help people better their life, expand, step into their greatness and remember who they are and that they matter. She created the C.A.L.M. System©, a series of tools that help people "Clear the C.R.A.P" Clear the Chaos, Restriction, Anger and Poverty – Get Clarity, Action, Love and Manifesting. She is also the author of *Healing Your Soul In A Chaotic World: Defying the Odds of Sanity and Survival.* She is known as a transmitter of love and joy.

You can reach Wendy at info@align-with-joy.com
or by calling 1-808-268-2407 in the USA.

www.align-with-joy.com

ABOUT WENDY LEE BALDWIN COACHING

If your soul is calling out, saying that it's time to let go of what's hurting and start transforming your life, then private mentoring might be right for you. Wendy offers private, one-on-one life changing sessions over the phone or video chat.

She understands that you might feel overwhelmed or scared about reaching out for help. Acknowledging how you feel is an important step in moving past the fear. Let an experienced professional help you from there. Connect with Wendy and share the part of your story that hurts and is yearning to heal, expand and be set free.

When mentoring with Wendy, she will gently and lovingly walk you through her proven transformational process that will be customized based on your unique needs. She also shares helpful tools and strategies designed to empower you. Her experiences, extensive training in multiple energetic healing methods as well as coaching certification and unique ability to hold safe, loving space makes your healing and transformational journey priceless. YOU are priceless.

Anyone wishing to work with her will have a no obligation complimentary 30 minute consultation first. It doesn't matter where you live. Age doesn't matter either. You're never too old or too young to let go of your old pain story and rewrite a new script for a magnificent future! You've suffered long enough.

Wendy Lee Baldwin is a Keynote speaker, Certified Wellness Coach, Certified Master Spiritual Coach, Holistic Healer and author of *Healing Your Soul In A Chaotic World: Defying the Odds of Sanity and Survival.*

Contact Wendy Lee Baldwin
to schedule your complimentary consultation.

1-808-268-2407 (Honolulu, Hawaii USA)

info@Align-With-Joy.com

www.Align-With-Joy.com

www.HealingYourSoulInAChaoticWorld.com

BOOK WENDY LEE BALDWIN TO SPEAK AT YOUR NEXT EVENT

When it comes to choosing a professional, passionate speaker at your next event, you won't find anyone like Wendy Lee Baldwin. She is known for speaking from her heart and soul, leaving audiences elevated, motivated and filled with hope and love. Her humor brings lightness and fun to serious topics which is something missing from most speakers.

Whether your group is 10 or 10,000, in North America or abroad, Wendy Lee Baldwin will deliver a customized message of inspiration, transformation and accomplishments. She shares real stories of her life and of others reclaiming their power and living life with gusto!

As a result, Wendy Lee Baldwin's speaking philosophy is to have fun, inspire and come from a state of love and gratitude. If you are looking for a memorable speaker who will leave you and your audience wanting more, then book Wendy Lee Baldwin today!

To see a highlight video of Wendy Lee Baldwin and find out whether she is available for your next meeting, visit her site at the address below. Then contact her by phone or email to schedule a complimentary pre-speech phone interview.

Wendy Lee Baldwin is a Keynote speaker, Certified Wellness Coach, Certified Master Spiritual Coach, Holistic Healer and author of *Healing Your Soul In A Chaotic World: Defying the Odds of Sanity and Survival.*

www.WendyLeeBaldwin.com
email info@align-with-joy.com
1-808-268-2407 in the USA

NOTES